H O L O C A U S T

Smoke to Flame

SEPTEMBER 1935 – DECEMBER 1938

By
Victoria Sherrow

Academic Editor:
Dr. William L. Shulman
President, Association of Holocaust Organizations
Director, Holocaust Resource Center & Archives, New York

Series Advisor:
Dr. Michael Berenbaum
President & CEO of Survivors of the
Shoah Visual History Foundation, Los Angeles

Series Editor:
Lisa Clyde Nielsen

Advisory Board:
Dr. Minton Goldman, Associate Professor of Political Science,
Northeastern University, Boston

Kathryn Schindler, Teacher, Laguna Niguel Middle School, California;
multicultural and tolerance educator

Kathryn Greenberg, Educational and public-administration specialist,
Chicago Department of Public Health, Division of School Health

Rachel Kubersky, BA Library Education, MPH

Joachim Kalter, Holocaust survivor

A   B L A C K B I R C H   P R E S S   B O O K
W O O D B R I D G E ,   C O N N E C T I C U T

Acknowledgments

Many people have given generously of their time and knowledge during the development of this series. We would like to thank the following people in particular: Genya Markon, and the staff at the United States Holocaust Memorial Museum Photo Archives—Leslie Swift, Sharon Muller, Alex Rossino, and Teresa Pollin—for their talented guidance; and Dr. Michael Berenbaum, currently President and CEO of the Survivors of the Shoah Visual History Foundation and formerly Director of the Research Institute at the U.S. Holocaust Memorial Museum, for his valuable editorial input and his enthusiastic support of our efforts.

Dr. William L. Shulman, President of the Association of Holocaust Organizations and Director of the Holocaust Resource Center & Archives at Queensborough Community College, merits special mention. As the series academic editor—as well as the compiler of Books 7 and 8—Dr. Shulman's guidance, insight, and dedication went far beyond the call of duty. His deep and thorough knowledge of the subject gave us all the critical perspective we needed to make this series a reality.

Published by Blackbirch Press, Inc.
260 Amity Road
Woodbridge, CT 06525

web site: http://www.blackbirch.com
e-mail: staff@blackbirch.com

©1998 Blackbirch Press, Inc.
First Edition

Printed in the United States of America

10 9 8 7 6 5 4 3 2 1

Cover: Austrian workers welcome the arrival of German troops in March 1938. Their sign reads "Sieg Heil to the Führer" (National Archives, Courtesy USHMM Photo Archives).

Library of Congress Cataloging-in-Publication Data

Sherrow, Victoria.
    Smoke to Flame: September 1935 to December 1938 / by Victoria Sherrow. —1st ed.
       p.   cm. — (Holocaust)
    Includes bibliographical references and index.
    ISBN 1-56711-201-3 (lib. bdg.: alk. paper)
    1. Jews—Germany—History—1933–1945—Juvenile literature. 2. Jews—Persecutions—Germany—Juvenile literature. 3. Germany—History—1933–1945—Juvenile literature. 4. Jews—Persecutions—Italy—Juvenile literature. 5. Italy—Ethnic relations—Juvenile literature. I. Title. II. Series: Holocaust (Woodbridge, Conn.)
DS135.G3315S53   1998
940.53'18'0943—dc21
                                                    96-52206
                                                        CIP
                                                         AC

CONTENTS

Preface

At the United States Holocaust Memorial Museum in Washington, D.C., a poignant documentary explores antisemitism and its role in the Holocaust. The film ends with these words:

THIS IS WHERE PREJUDICE CAN LEAD.

That somber warning has guided our work on this series.

The task of creating a series of books on the Holocaust seemed, at first, straightforward enough: We would develop an in-depth account of one of the most complex and compelling periods in human history.

But it quickly became clear to us that, on an emotional level, this series would not be straightforward at all. Indeed, the more work we did, the more we realized just how this subject wraps itself around everyone it touches. As we discussed content with our authors and advisors and began to select photographs and other documents for reproduction, several unanticipated and complicated issues arose.

The first major issue was pivotal, in that our decision would guide the content of the books: How should we choose to define the very term *Holocaust?* Many scholars of the Holocaust believe that the term should be used exclusively in reference to the approximately 6 million European Jews who were murdered by Nazis and their collaborators between 1933 and 1945. This is because no other group was singled out so systematically and relentlessly for genocide. Should the perhaps 4 million non-Jewish victims of the period—the Soviet prisoners of war, Romani (Gypsies), Jehovah's Witnesses, German and Austrian male homosexuals, and other groups—be discussed on the same level as the Jews? Ultimately—in philosophical agreement with the U.S. Holocaust Memorial Museum—we decided to focus our discussion primarily on the Jews but also to report the experiences of other victims.

Our second major decision had to do with how to present the material. How explicit should the books be in their written descriptions and photographic records of what was done to the victims? Perhaps never before have the brutalities of war and the consequences of prejudice and hatred been so extensively chronicled; perhaps never so eloquently and, at the same time, in such painful detail.

On this issue, we decided we would chronicle what happened, but try not to shock or horrify. Learning about the Holocaust should be disturbing—but there is a delicate line between informative realism and sensationalism. The most brutal accounts and documentation of the Holocaust can be found in many other sources; we believe that in our series, much of this story will be revealed through the powerful and moving images we have selected.

Yet another difficult issue was raised by our educational advisors: Was the Holocaust truly a singular historical event, uniquely qualified for such detailed study as is provided in this series? That it was an extraordinary period in history, there can be no denial—despite some misguided people's efforts to the contrary. Certainly, never before had an entire nation organized its power and mobilized itself so efficiently for the sole purpose of destroying human life. Yet the Holocaust was not unique in terms of the number of people murdered; nor was it unique in the brutality of the hatred on which it fed.

A subject such as this raises many questions. How could the Holocaust have happened? Could it have been prevented? How can we keep this from happening again? We have done our best to explore the questions we feel are most central. Ultimately, however, the most compelling questions to emerge from learning about the Holocaust are for each individual reader to answer.

Foreword

There is a paradox in the study of the Holocaust: The more distant we are from the Event, the more interest seems to grow. In the immediate aftermath of the Holocaust, horrific images were played in movie theaters on newsreels, which was how people saw the news in an era before television. Broadcasting on CBS radio, famed newscaster Edward R. Murrow said:

Permit me to tell you what you would have seen and heard had you been with me on Thursday. It will not be pleasant listening. If you are at lunch or have no appetite to hear of what Germans have done, now is a good time to turn off your radio, for I propose to tell you of Buchenwald.

Murrow described the sights and sounds of what he had experienced in the immediate aftermath of liberation, and his audience was appropriately horrified. Action was required, trials were soon held—an accounting for a deed that was beyond human comprehension, a crime beyond a name, that we now call the "Holocaust."

Shortly thereafter, interest waned. Other topics of the era took center stage—the Cold War, the Berlin blockade, the Korean War—and it seemed for a time that the Holocaust would be forgotten. In retrospect, we can surmise that the silence was a necessary response to such catastrophe. Distance was needed before we could look back and muster enough courage to confront an event so terrible.

No one could have imagined that, half a century after the Holocaust, museums such as the United States Holocaust Memorial Museum would be built and would attract millions of visitors each year. No one, too, would have guessed that films such as *Schindler's List* would be seen by tens of millions of people throughout the world. No one could have foreseen that thousands of books would be published on the subject and courses in schools all over the world would be taught—that interest in this horrible chapter of history would intensify rather than recede with the passage of time.

Why study the Holocaust?

The answer is simple: Because it happened!

An event of such magnitude, a state-sponsored annihilation of an entire people—men, women, and children— must be confronted. Some people have portrayed the Holocaust as an aberration, a world apart from the ordinary world in which we dwell. Even the most eloquent of survivors, Elie Wiesel, calls it the "Kingdom of Night." Yet, to me the Holocaust is not an aberration, but an expression in the extreme of a common thread that runs through our civilization. And thus, not to confront the Event is not to probe the deep darkness that is possible within our world.

Because it happened, we must seek to understand the anguish of the victims— the men, women, and children who faced death and had impossible choices to make, and who could do so little to determine their fate. And we must seek to understand the neutrality and indifference of the bystanders around the world; and what caused the Allies—who were fighting a full-scale world war against the Germans and other Axis powers—to fail to address the "second war," the war against the Jews.

We must also seek to understand the all-too-few non-Jewish heroes of the Holocaust—the men, women, and children who opened their homes and their hearts and provided a haven for the victims; a place to sleep, a crust of bread, a kind word, a hiding place. What makes such goodness possible? Why were they immune to the infection of evil?

We must understand that the Holocaust did not begin with mass killing. Age-old prejudice led to discrimination, discrimination led to persecution, persecution to incarceration, incarceration to annihilation. And mass murder, which culminated with the killing of approximately 6 million Jews, did not begin with the Jews—nor did it encompass only the Jews. The state-sponsored murder of the physically and mentally disabled was a precursor to the Holocaust. It was in that killing process that gas chambers and crematoria were developed and refined, and the staff of the death camps were trained. Romani (commonly but incorrectly referred to as Gypsies) were killed alongside the Jews. Jehovah's Witnesses, German and Austrian male homosexuals, political prisoners and dissidents were also incarcerated in concentration camps, where many were murdered. Gentile and Jewish Poles were subjected to decimation and destruction of their national identity. Though many Jews suffered alone, abandoned and forgotten by the world, they were not the only ones to die.

The study of the Holocaust is not easy. We are often unclear about whose history is being taught: German history, Jewish history, American history, European history. And to understand it, we need to understand more than history. Other disciplines are essential, such as psychology and sociology, political science, philosophy and theology, and, most especially, ethics. When we study the Holocaust, we are forced to face evil, to confront experiences that are horrific and destructive. And even despite the tools of all these disciplines, we still may not understand. Comprehension may elude us.

With the renewed interest in the Holocaust—especially in North America—we have seen that the study of all these deaths is actually in the service of life; the study of evil actually strengthens decency and goodness. For us as free citizens, confronting this European event brings us a new recognition of the principles of constitutional democracy: a belief in equality and equal justice under law; a commitment to pluralism and toleration; a determination to restrain government by checks and balances and by the constitutional protection of "inalienable rights"; and a struggle for human rights as a core value.

The Holocaust shatters the myth of innocence and, at the same time, has implications for the exercise of power. Those who wrestle with its darkness know it can happen again—even in the most advanced, most cultured, most "civilized" of societies. But, if we are faithful to the best of human values, the most sterling of our traditions, then we can have confidence that it "won't happen here." These truths are not self-evident; they are precarious and, therefore, even more precious.

The Holocaust has implications for us as individuals. As we read these books, we can't help but ask ourselves, "What would I have done?" "If I were a Jew, would I have had the courage to resist—spiritually or militarily—and when?" "Would I have had the wisdom and the ability to flee to a place that offered a haven?" "Do I have a friend who would offer me a place of shelter, a piece of bread, a moment of refuge?" "What could I have done to protect my family, to preserve my life?"

We can't offer easy answers because the options were few, the pressures extreme, the conditions unbearable, and the stakes ultimate—life or death.

We may also ask ourselves even more difficult questions: "What prejudices do I have?" "Do I treat all people with full human dignity?" "Am I willing to discriminate against some, to scapegoat others?" "Am I certain—truly certain—that I could not be a killer? That I would not submit to the pressures of conformity and participate in horrible deeds or, worse yet, embrace a belief that makes me certain—absolutely certain—that I am right and the others are wrong? That my cause is just and the other is an enemy who threatens me, who must be eliminated?" These are questions you will ask as you read these books—ask, but not answer.

Perhaps, in truth, the more intensely you read these books, the less certainty you will have in offering your personal answer. Premature answers are often immature answers. Good questions invite one to struggle with basic values.

The central theme of the story of the Holocaust is not regeneration and rebirth, goodness or resistance, liberation or justice, but, rather, death and destruction, dehumanization and devastation, and above all, loss.

The killers were "civilized" men and women of an advanced culture. They were both ordinary and extraordinary, a true cross-section of the men and women of Germany, its allies, and their collaborators, as well as the best and the brightest. In these volumes, those deeds will be seen, as will the evolution of policy, the expansion of the power of the state, and technological and scientific murders unchecked by moral, social, religious, or political constraints. Whether restricted to the past or a harbinger of the future, the killers demonstrated that systematic mass destruction is possible. Under contemporary conditions, the execution of such a policy would only be easier.

The Holocaust transforms our understanding. It shatters faith—religious faith in God and secular faith in human goodness. Its truth has been told not to provide answers, but to raise questions. To live conscientiously in its aftermath, one must confront the reality of radical evil and its past triumphs. At the same time, we must fight against that evil and its potential triumphs in the future.

The call from the victims—from the world of the dead—is to remember. From the survivors, initial silence has given way to testimony. The burden of memory has been transmitted and thus shared. From scholars, philosophers, poets, and artists—those who were there and those who were not—we hear the urgency of memory, its agony and anguish, its meaning and the absence of meaning. To live in our age, one must face the void.

Israel Ba'al Shem Tov, the founder of Hasidism, once said:

In forgetfulness is the root of exile.
In remembrance, the seed of
redemption.

His fears of forgetting, we understand all too well.

Whether we can share his hope of remembrance is uncertain.

Still, it is up to us to create that hope.

Michael Berenbaum
Survivors of the Shoah
Visual History Foundation
Los Angeles, California

"Hypnotized"

For many centuries Germany had been an international center of culture and learning. The nation had produced some of the world's most outstanding philosophers, scientists, artists, writers, and musicians. Great philosophers and writers such as Goethe and Schiller, and composers such as Beethoven, Bach, and Brahms were just a few of Germany's native sons. Given this long-standing and rich cultural tradition, most Germans were proud of their civilized heritage.

During the 1930s, however, this "civilized" nation was radically changed. Throughout Germany, there were harsh attacks on democracy. Vile words were hurled at certain groups of people because of their race, nationality, mental or physical disability, political beliefs, or religion.

Adolf Hitler addresses the crowd assembled in Nuremberg, Germany, during Reich Party Day ceremonies in September 1935.

These ugly sentiments flowed from the very core of the government itself, under the dictator Adolf Hitler. In 1933, Hitler's militaristic National Socialist German Workers' Party—called the Nazi Party—rose to power. After proclaiming himself *Führer* ("leader") of Germany, Hitler pledged to lead the nation into a glorious future, an era in its history that he called the Third Reich. This empire, declared Hitler, would last for at least a thousand years.

The Nazis managed to rise quickly to power during a time of political unrest and severe economic decline in Germany, following World War I. At first, many Germans ignored, criticized, even ridiculed Hitler. As he gained control, certain political parties, churches, labor unions, military leaders, and pacifists opposed him more strongly. But these groups were relatively small and did not unite effectively against the Nazis. Nor did the majority of German citizens.

Rise of a Dictator

As time went on, millions of Germans came to support, even idolize Adolf Hitler. He was a powerful speaker who vowed to solve Germany's problems. A severe, worldwide depression had started in 1929, and an unprecedented number of Germans were unemployed and desperately poor. They craved jobs and security, which the Nazis promised to supply. Businesspeople also supported Hitler, because he strongly opposed the Communist Party and its aim of giving more power to workers.

Hitler also appealed to the Germans' strong sense of national pride, which had been wounded by their humiliating defeat in World War I (1914–1918). During that war, approximately 10 million soldiers and civilians died. To punish Germany for its aggression and to cripple its military, the Allies forced German leaders to sign the Treaty of Versailles in 1919. The treaty required Germany to strictly limit its military, give up lands in France and Poland, and pay billions of dollars in reparations—payments—to help rebuild the nations that had been devastated in the war. The

Europe in 1935, Before German Expansion Under Hitler Began

terms of this treaty—and the fact that Germany was forced to sign it—caused bitter resentment among Germans.

Exploiting this anger, Hitler offered German citizens easy excuses for Germany's problems. In doing that, he used Communists and especially Jews as prime scapegoats. Hitler claimed that the Jews (who numbered about 500,000, less than 1 percent of Germany's population) had caused the war, unemployment, hunger, and poverty. In fact, some 100,000 German Jews had fought for the Germans in World War I; thousands had earned medals for bravery, and more than 12,000 had died. Yet, Hitler blamed Jews for Germany's defeat. He even claimed that an international Jewish conspiracy planned to take over the world. At a political rally in Munich, Hitler called Jews "murderers, Communists, and thieves," saying, "We are the result of the distress for which others have been responsible."

Dynamic. . . mesmerizing. . . thrilling. . . insane. . . terrifying. . . shrill—all of these words have been used to describe Adolf Hitler. By 1935, he had been spreading his message of hate for nearly 15 years. Often, he told Germans that they were destined to become a world power, a "master race" that would rise above all others. This superior "race" would include only "Aryans." The word *Aryan* had several meanings—it referred to an ancient Indo–European people but was also used to describe a group of languages spoken in Europe. Hitler applied the term to people with fair coloring whose ancestors had originated in certain parts of Northern Europe. In his mind, most other "races"—as he incorrectly called them—were inferior, including Romani (often but incorrectly called Gypsies), Slavic peoples (from Poland, Czechoslovakia, Bulgaria, Serbia, Croatia, Ukraine, and Russia), and Africans. Above all, however, Hitler despised the Jews, who were actually a religious group, not a "race."

Although troubled, most Jews initially thought Hitler would not gain much support. When he became Germany's leader in 1933, some Jews were alarmed enough to leave the country, but the vast majority stayed. They thought Hitler's regime would collapse as people rejected his false ideas and divisive racism. And, after all, Germany was their country, too.

Contrary to their hopes, Hitler steadily gained public support. Germans flocked to hear speeches in which the *Führer* warned about "threats" to Germany, both from within and from abroad. Hitler demanded more *Lebensraum*—"living space," or land, for the German people. To achieve this, he proposed the invasion and domination of neighboring countries. And he spoke endlessly of his desire to eliminate Jews from Germany.

At first, Hitler's speeches and policies were not so aggressive. During the early 1930s, Hitler claimed that he sought peace and friendship with other nations. But this was just a deception. While Germany quietly built up its military, other nations ignored or misjudged the Nazi threat. Most Germans dreaded another war and convinced themselves that Hitler would keep the peace.

Total Control

By 1935, the Nazi government controlled virtually all areas of German life—politics, the economy, the legal system and courts, the police, the media, education, sports, and the arts. Hitler was chancellor, president, and commander of the army, and he demanded complete obedience. This one man's grip on his country was so strong that military men recited oaths of allegiance to Hitler, rather than to the nation or to the law.

Josef Goebbels, the minister of Public Enlightenment and Propaganda, developed a massive propaganda machine to ensure that the German people would support the Nazis' goals. Goebbels essentially decided what Germans could see, hear, read, write, print, and study.

The government strictly censored all the media. Modern art, whether by Jewish artists or others, was banned. Between 1933 and 1935, millions of books were burned by the Nazis. They banned books written by Jews, including poet Heinrich Heine, or works that contained ideas the Nazis viewed as "un-German" or offensive. By 1935, more than 12,000 books had been officially outlawed. Some famous writers fled Germany; so did Jewish and non-Jewish musicians, filmmakers, scientists, artists, teachers, and others who could no longer work freely. Among them were author Thomas Mann, a Gentile (non-Jew), and Jewish scientist Albert Einstein.

Max Von Der Grun, who was born in rural Germany in 1926, later wrote about the constant propaganda during those years:

Every day the people were fed with proverbs from the Führer. . . . *Every day one heard or saw [our rulers] everywhere: in the press, which always conformed to the party line, in the radio, in films, and in the newsreels, which in those days were as popular as the daily television news programs are today. We saw Hitler at banquets and parades, both of which events took place somewhere every day. . . . Hypnotized by flags, banners, speeches, and marching feet, the German people...were left no time to think about why the whole production was being staged. Like everything else, the music, too, was simple and easy to understand: hiking songs, folksongs, war songs, songs of the new Germany—and constantly the music of marching bands.*

Attacks on Jews

Most Nazi propaganda attacked Jews. For centuries, Jews had occasionally been the victims of religious intolerance, not only in Germany but in many other places. During intense periods of persecution in Europe, Jews had been forced to live in ghettos (walled-off parts of towns) and had been barred from owning land, voting, holding public office, and pursuing certain jobs and professions. Pogroms—group attacks on Jews and their property—had occasionally taken place. Jews had long struggled for the right to practice their religion freely and for fair—if not equal—treatment under the law.

In Germany, Jews were formally granted full citizenship only in 1871, although they had lived there for many centuries (longer than the Goths and Franks, whom Hitler called "true Germans"). Jews had contributed to all areas of German life—science, music, education, literature, art, commerce, military service. They were integrated into all parts of society and viewed themselves as ordinary and loyal German citizens. Now the Nazi government was attacking them, persecuting them under a banner of religious and racial intolerance.

"Hatred, Burning Hatred"

Through their propaganda, the Nazis hoped to drive Jews out of Germany and persuade other people not to care when Jews were abused. The most unrelenting propaganda was meant to influence young people, soldiers, war veterans, and paramilitary groups (armed men who were prone to use violence against their enemies). Many of these Germans became soldiers or members of the Nazi secret police—the Gestapo. They were people willing to commit brutal acts against Jews and other supposed "enemies" of the state at the request of their leaders.

As soon as the Nazis seized power, they set out to control the behavior of Germans of all ages. Because they realized that young people's minds were especially vulnerable, Nazis targeted schools—from elementary through university—to build support for the Third Reich. Each day, schoolchildren had to recite this verse, glorifying Hitler:

Führer, *my* Führer, *bequeathed to me by the Lord,*
Protect and preserve me as long as I live.

After banning parent–teacher groups, the government installed new textbooks that glamorized Nazi characters and promoted prejudice, mostly against Jews. Every subject was used to stir up jealousy and hatred. For instance, one math problem labeled Jews as "aliens in Germany." Students were asked to calculate the percentage of "aliens," using numbers of Jews for the solution.

School routines and rituals also reinforced Nazism. Children were required daily to recite Nazi pledges, sing Nazi songs, and give the Nazi salute, in which the arm was held straight out and raised with fingers held

Hitler Youth

together. Flags with swastikas—bent-arm crosses that the Nazis adopted as their symbol—hung in every schoolroom along with portraits of Hitler. Students who approved of the government were rewarded with praise and good grades; those who did not were punished.

Outside of school, the government saw to it that children had games and pastimes that reflected and reinforced Nazi ideas. One of these was a board game called "Get the Jews Out!" The directions told players to take care when throwing the dice so they could collect large numbers of Jews, whom they could then "throw out" of Germany to win the game. It sold millions of copies during the 1930s.

When not in school, young people were exposed to more Nazi indoctrination through various kinds of Hitler Youth groups. By the end of 1938, there were four Hitler Youth groups, divided according to age, with some 8.7 million members. About half of the members were girls. Besides taking part in camping trips and sports, the Hitler Youth spent time marching, receiving paramilitary training, holding field exercises, and shooting rifles.

Speaking of his plan to promote antisemitism, Hitler said, "Hatred, burning hatred—that is what we want to pour into the souls of our millions of fellow Germans until the flame of rage ignites our Germany and avenges the corrupters of our nation."

Jews came to dread hearing Hitler's voice on the radio and Nazi speechmakers on the street. They felt fear, disgust, and confusion as "brown-shirts"—brown-uniformed Nazis—or groups of Hitler Youth marched by, often singing the *Horst Wessel*, a Nazi anthem with lyrics that glorified the killing of Jews.

Among those who felt this ever-growing fear was Netti Golde Dessau, who grew up in Frankfurt. The people she knew called Hitler's ideas "crazy." Dessau recalled listening to Hitler:

He was an enormously strong speaker and really had a way of arousing people. . . . I always felt if I did nothing wrong, nothing would happen to me. I couldn't understand the idea that people would persecute us just because we were Jewish.

The Nazi regime destroyed the lives of German Jews bit by bit, depriving them of jobs, businesses, and education. By 1935, Jews could no longer work as judges, as university teachers, or hold banking and railroad positions. Nor could they serve in the army or navy. The number of Jewish students at universities was strictly limited. Streets named after prominent Jews were renamed. The names of the more than 12,000 Jewish German soldiers who had died during World War I were erased from war memorials.

Not only were they cast out of German life; Jews were also viciously insulted at every turn. Scathing articles that featured crude antisemitic cartoons hurled hatred at them from newsstands. Antisemitic signs and posters filled more and more space on street corners and on private and public buildings, even schools. Jews entering a restaurant would most likely be sent away with the words, "We don't serve Jews." Newspaper articles warned non-Jews that associating with Jews was "a sin against your German *Volk* [folk, or people] and its future."

In Jewish homes throughout Germany, people wondered: What next? How bad will it get? Surely, the government will change. Surely people will realize the Nazis are abusing power and treating people inhumanely.

Go or stay? This became the urgent question for nearly every Jew in Germany. Some of those who remained grew hopeful when 1934 and the early part of 1935 brought fewer new actions and laws against Jews.

But then, ominous signs appeared. In 1935, the government began ignoring letters and petitions from Jews who were documenting abuses and asking for fair treatment under the law. In one petition, Jewish leaders in Berlin (the German capital) pointed out that German Jews were "rooted in Germany and its culture" and that actions against them "work not only against the Jews but against the well-being of Germany." They noted that Jews were a small minority in Germany; their numbers had actually declined since 1800. Besides, they argued, persecuting Jews could damage Germany's reputation around the world.

Despite these pleas, violence against Jews and their places of business increased. For many German Jews, this atmosphere of increasing violence meant that staying in their country was no longer an option. By 1935, some 50,000 German Jews had already left Germany. In July 1935, Jews were beaten on the streets of Berlin during anti-Jewish riots. Articles in the Nazi press were now filled with outrageous lies, as when the newspaper *Der Stürmer* ("The Attacker") ran a story accusing Jews of a plot to kill non-Jews.

By autumn 1935, the sounds of hatred were growing louder and more persistent. A vast tragedy was unfolding, in stops and starts, not always with a clear direction. Jews were being isolated, treated as inferior, and accused of trying to ruin Germany and even the world. Soon they would lose civil rights and the chance to earn a living. Life would become increasingly grim as the Nazis used the full force of the government to persecute millions of people, young and old, solely because they were Jews.

"We Are Already Being Watched"

The Nazis had gradually been taking away the Jews' freedoms and making them second-class citizens. But in Germany in September 1935, the Jews' remaining rights were stripped away. It was then that the Reichstag (German Parliament) met in the city of Nuremberg and passed laws severely restricting the Jews. They were made not just second-class citizens, but non-citizens— merely "subjects" of the Nazi regime.

German Jews had a wide range of religious beliefs and practices. In their religious practices, some were very observant; others were less so. Intermarriage over the years had produced families with both Christian and Jewish members. Some Jews had changed to another religion; some practiced no religion at all.

Many German Jews in the early 1930s enjoyed the comfort and success of middle-class life. This montage shows a group of Jewish friends and family from Leipzig at work, play, and celebrating the happiness of special occasions.

Nazi leaders ignored these differences. To suit their purposes, they defined "Jewishness" not as a religion but in terms of "race," based on who had Jewish "blood." This idea, of course, had no scientific merit; people around the world have the same kinds of blood, made up of the same chemicals. But Adolf Hitler told people that there was something different and "inferior" about the blood of Jews, as well as Romani, Africans, Slavs, and other groups. He said that "true Germans," whom he called Aryans, were a pure-blooded race, "superior" to others.

A Question of "Blood"

The first of the so-called Nuremberg Laws—officially designated the Reich Citizenship Laws—were passed on September 15, 1935. One section declared that only persons with "German or kindred blood" could be called "citizens of the Reich." Only these citizens would have full political rights, including the right to vote or hold office.

Also enacted was the Law for the Protection of German Blood and German Honor. It said, "Marriages between Jews and citizens of German or related blood are forbidden. Marriages performed despite this ban are invalid, even if performed abroad to avoid this law." This ban was extended to include marriages between Jews and non-Jews that already existed.

Jews could no longer employ non-Jewish women under age 45 as servants. This law was meant to prevent any possible sexual relations between female servants of child-bearing age and a Jewish employer. Jews could not fly the

This example of Nazi racial propaganda depicts Jews as "bastard sons" of Asian and Negroid peoples.

German flag or display the national colors. The penalties for breaking these laws included imprisonment and fines. Henry Frank, then a teenager in Berlin, recalled, "All of a sudden, we were no longer considered German."

On October 18, 1935, Hitler introduced more such laws. Henceforth, no German citizens could marry until the government determined that they could not pass on any hereditary diseases—mental or physical problems that run in families. He said these would "ensure the continued derivation of the German people from healthy stock."

Later, the Nazis would use these laws to murder people whom they labeled as "inferior" and believed were not fit to live. And, in pursuit of their "master race," the Nazis also subjected some people to sterilization—surgery that prevented them from ever having children.

New laws handed down on November 15 affected people whose ancestors were both Christian and Jewish, people known as *Mischlinge* (a derogatory term meaning "mongrels"). These laws defined degrees of "Jewishness." Under these laws, anyone who had two or more Jewish grandparents was fully Jewish.

Coping With the New Laws

Although they were deeply concerned, most Jews tried to adjust to life under the Nuremberg Laws. As a people, they had managed to survive for many centuries, building strong communities despite occasional persecution. Their religious traditions emphasized reason and justice; many believed these ideals would soon triumph over Nazism. Some also felt a responsibility to stay and struggle for the moral right of German Jews to remain in their homeland.

A few people even felt relief when the laws were passed. They hoped that, because the government had now clearly spelled out its policy, random attacks and arrests of Jews would stop. Also, the laws did not ban Jews from making a living or owning property in Germany, which some viewed as a good sign.

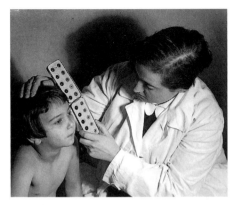

Throughout Germany, "scientific" examinations were done of eye color, nose width, and other "racial" features to determine who possessed what Nazis considered "inferior" and "superior" traits.

Jews tried to maintain their family life, work, culture, and religious organizations in this hostile environment. Articles in the Jewish press urged Jews to support one another during these grim times and to remain proud of their heritage. In response, many people took a more active part in their religion, and rabbis (religious leaders) held extra services to accommodate them.

The Nuremberg Laws strained human relationships on nearly all levels. Many non-Jews broke business ties with Jews. Old friendships came to an abrupt end. One Jewish woman, for example, stopped meeting a group of friends at a café in her hometown. She said, "I did not want to cause difficulties for my friends as a result of my presence." Other Jews urged non-Jews to stay away in order to avoid trouble. One woman warned a dear friend who came to visit, "Don't come in, we are already being watched."

By isolating Jews, it was even easier for the Nazis to spread lies and to dehumanize Jews, constantly telling people that they were a "problem." In passing the Nuremberg Laws, Nazi leaders had shown that they were willing to use government powers to persecute Jews however they wished. German Jews now had no security.

J for Jude

As 1935 ended, Jews faced ever more restrictions. Jewish doctors could no longer treat non-Jewish patients. Lawyers could not represent non-Jews, nor could Jewish musicians or actors perform for non-Jewish audiences. Jewish shops were marked by Nazis with the letter *J*, for *Jude* ("Jew") and six-pointed Stars of David, Jewish symbols, were painted on buildings owned by Jews.

The Nazis also dismissed many Jewish teachers and began the process of filling schools with Nazi Party members. One Jewish teacher told how she lost her job one morning. The principal of her school stopped her in the hallway and led her to his office:

"The Shame of Nuremberg"

As more and more abuses were heaped on German Jews, foreign observers—including many news correspondents based in Germany—expressed dismay. The *New York Herald Tribune* published an attack on the German government called "The Shame of Nuremberg." The *Times* of London called the Nuremberg Laws a "complete disinheritance and segregation of Jewish citizens." The African-American educator and activist Mary McLeod Bethune led a civil-rights group that denounced the Nuremberg Laws and asked U.S. government leaders to formally and publicly condemn the Nazis.

A few people sensed impending disaster. One of them was Eric Mills, the British commissioner for Migration and Statistics in Palestine (a small territory in the Middle East, part of which would later become the State of Israel). Palestine was then under British control. Mills had made several visits to Berlin in order to handle matters relating to Jewish immigration to Palestine, a place where many Jews hoped to settle. In a letter to his government in November 1935, Mills wrote:

> While before I went to Germany, I knew that the Jewish situation was bad, I had not realized as I now do that the fate of German Jews is a tragedy. . . . The Jew is to be eliminated and the state has no regard for the manner of his elimination.

The Nazis responded as they had in the past when their policies were attacked: They threatened to take even harsher measures against Jews if any nation threatened Germany or boycotted German goods. During the 1930s, Nazi officials watched closely the reaction of the foreign press and foreign leaders. After a while, it became clear that, while foreigners might criticize them, no nation was willing to take decisive action to stop Germany from persecuting Jews. In many ways, the Nazis took this lack of action as a tacit approval from the rest of the world. With this approval, they felt even more justified in escalating their persecutions.

When we were seated, he said in a serious, embarrassed tone of voice, he had orders to ask me not to go into my classroom. I probably knew, he said, that I was not permitted to teach anymore at a German school. . . . I rode home. . . . In the afternoon, colleagues, pupils, their mothers came, some in a sad mood, others angry with their country, lovely bouquets of flowers, large and small, in their arms. In the evening, the little house was full of fragrance and colors, like for a funeral, I thought. . . the funeral of my time teaching at a German public school.

"Nothing Weak or Tender"

As 1936 began, more people joined the Nazi Party. Many were eager supporters of Hitler's new Reich. Others joined for practical reasons—to keep their jobs or get better ones. Some joined simply out of fear.

Starting at age 10, young people were pressed to join one of the four Hitler Youth groups, something that would be required by law of all those not labeled "inferior" in 1936. Hitler had a clear plan for German youths. He said:

All weakness must be hammered out. . . . I want a youth that is violent, masterful, intrepid, cruel. Young people must be all these things. They must endure pain. There must be nothing weak or tender in them.

Speaking to the Reichstag in December 1938, Hitler stressed that all Germans must take part in some Nazi organization at every stage of life. "These young people will learn nothing else but how to think German and act German," he said. "They will never be free again, not their whole lives long."

Irmgard Lochner, who grew up in Germany and later moved to the United States, joined the Hitler Youth. She recalled:

I must say I liked it because it was very sports and music oriented, but we knew from my parents and from the [Church] that this was something bad. So, I joined the Catholic youth group, too.

Lochner, with bitter memories of the war years, said her family later regretted joining the Nazi Party. But, she said, "It was an advantage to join. . . . I mean you could just go on living without being molested in any way."

Voices of Dissent

Some Germans criticized or ridiculed Hitler among themselves. A number of people listened to foreign radio stations and kept banned books, often hiding them in attics.

By 1935, Catholic and Protestant officials in Germany seemed resigned to co-existing with the Nazis. Most religious leaders did not openly rebuke Hitler or urge people to oppose him, although some local clergy gave sermons criticizing him. To stop them, uniformed Nazis began attending church services.

Among the people who spoke out against the government was Ernst Wiechert, a well-known writer. In 1935, during a speech at the University of Munich, Wiechert said bluntly:

> It is quite possible for a people to cease to distinguish between justice and injustice. It is also possible that such a people may for a time win a gladiator's glory. But such a people already stands on the brink of a precipice, and the law decreeing its destruction has already been written.

But by that time, public protest against the Nazis was rare. Strict laws and the ever-present police quashed dissent. The Gestapo and SS (the *Schutzstaffel*, Hitler's personal security men) were free to arrest people on any charges they wished. SS men wore a skull and crossbones on their uniforms and bore daggers inscribed, "My honor is loyalty." They pledged obedience until death to Hitler. Informers were everywhere. Many Germans "denounced" others to the police. Children were urged to report anyone, including their parents, for anti-Nazi remarks or activities.

People who stepped out of line faced arrest, interrogation, even death. Quite often, those questioned by Nazi police were

----- "I Will Go When I Am the Last Jew Alive in Germany" -----

When Rabbi Samuel Baeck died in 1912 in Lissa, Germany, the bells of the town hall and Christian churches tolled in sympathy for the loss of the Jewish community's spiritual leader. It was quite a different Germany in the 1930s, however, when Baeck's son, Rabbi Leo Baeck, headed the Berlin Synagogue.

From the outset, Rabbi Baeck was deeply concerned about the rise of Hitler's antisemitic government. As early as 1934, Baeck recognized the need to emigrate from Germany. He said of Jewish youth, "The only thing to do is to get them out." After the Nuremberg Laws were passed, Baeck wrote a sermon to be read at every German synagogue on Yom Kippur, the holiest day of the year for Jews. This prayer lamented the lies being told about the Jewish people and said: "We stand before our God...we bow to Him, and we stand upright and erect before man."

The Gestapo arrested Baeck for reading the sermon. In response, 12 American Protestant ministers sent a letter of protest to the German Embassy. It said:

> ...any government which permits or condones such actions toward religious leaders—whether they are Jewish or Christian—cannot expect the leaders of religious life in other lands to take seriously its claims to be friendly to ethics, religion, and the standards of civilization.

Because of his worldwide reputation, Rabbi Baeck had many chances to leave before and during the war. Baeck refused, saying, "I will go when I am the last Jew alive in Germany."

In 1943, at age 69, Rabbi Baeck was sent to Theresienstadt, where he continued to inspire people with his courage and humanity.

physically abused. Some dissenters were sent to concentration (labor or work) camps. (In 1938, Ernst Wiechert was sent to one such camp, Buchenwald, for criticizing the Nazis. He survived and later wrote about the camp in *Der Totenwald*—"The Forest of the Dead.")

By 1935, several concentration camps were operating, with thousands of political prisoners trapped inside their walls. They included members of the Communist and Social Democrat Parties and others who had opposed Hitler and wanted changes in the government. Also imprisoned were Protestant and Catholic clergy who had angered the Nazis.

Hitler's New Germany

As 1935 neared its end, more Jews had lost hope and left Germany. Laws banned those who fled from taking much money or many belongings. They had to sell their homes and businesses for ridiculously low prices; sometimes they even had to give them away for nothing. These enterprises were then handed out to government officials or Nazi supporters as rewards for loyalty.

Meanwhile, many German men found jobs in factories that made supplies and arms for the ever-growing army. In direct violation of the Versailles Treaty, Hitler was building up the army and re-arming Germany. Still other Germans began working in the Nazi government and its police organizations, or they built roads that would later transport German tanks beyond Germany's borders. Having banned all labor unions, the Nazis also proceeded to decrease wages and increase working hours while limiting prices. In these ways, they claimed to have "improved" the German economy.

By the end of 1935, approximately 75,000 of Germany's 500,000 Jews had left. Of these refugees, about 30,000 went to Palestine, and 9,000 settled in the United States. Several thousand went to Great Britain, while others moved to Canada, Australia, and South Africa. Some Jews stayed in Europe, hoping for better lives in France, Belgium, Holland, Czechoslovakia, or Austria.

As 1936 loomed on the horizon, the Nazis had millions of devoted supporters, and their base was growing. Another phase of Hitler's master plan had now been realized. He had successfully ignited violent feelings in his people that would soon erupt into ever more vicious and destructive acts.

This Jewish-owned rubberware shop in Frankfurt—Gummi-Weil—was seized and "Aryanized." It was renamed Stamm & Bassermann.

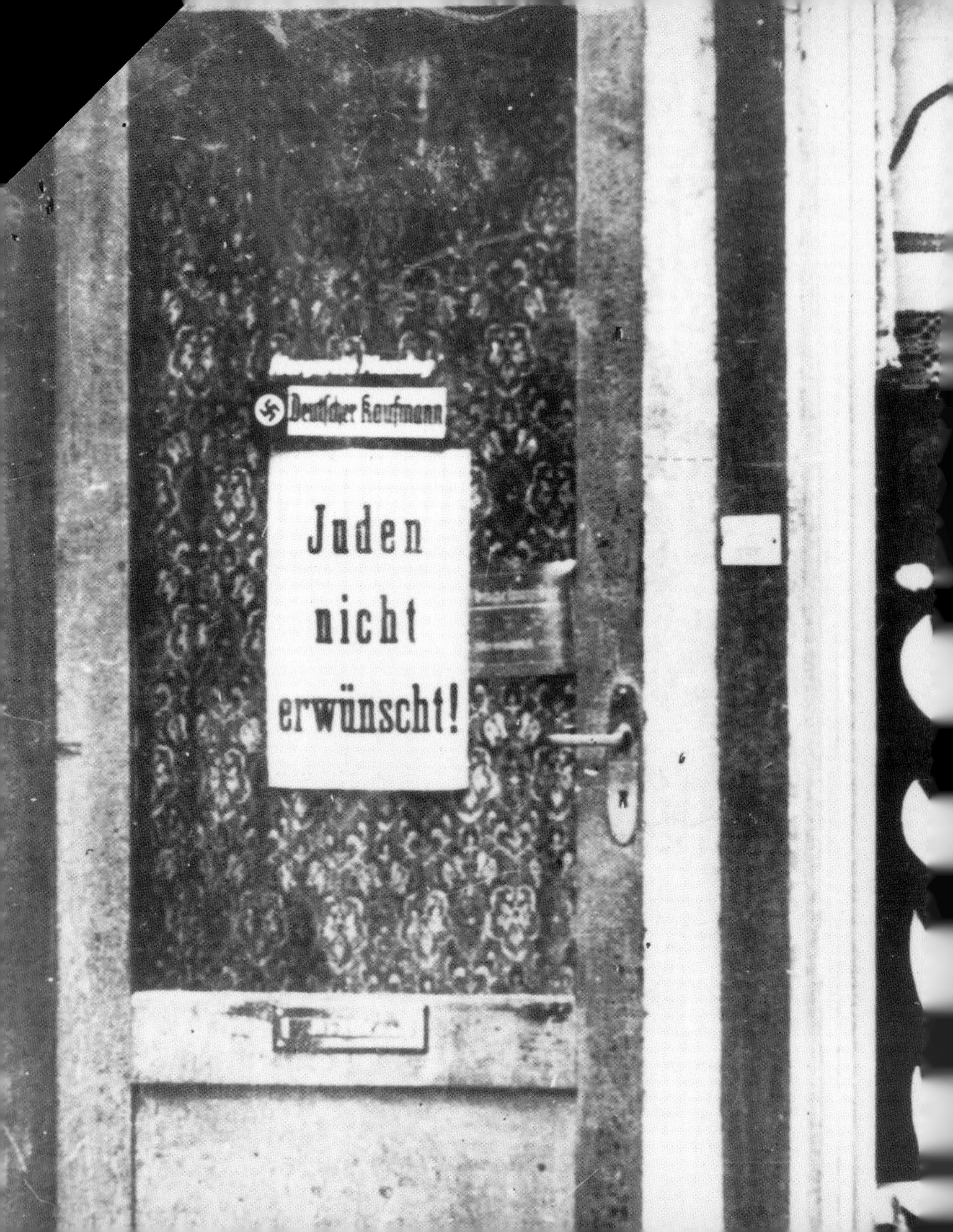
Deutscher Kaufmann
Juden nicht erwünscht!

"Inhuman Indifference"

During the early months of 1936, German Jews faced more danger and uncertainty. Laws, boycotts, and social pressure were forcing them out of their professions and businesses at an increased pace. Stores and public places of all kinds were told to post signs that read JEWS NOT WELCOME or JEWS NOT ADMITTED. Some signs offered up these menacing words: JEWS ENTER AT THEIR OWN RISK.

Poverty Spreads

Within a few months after the Nuremberg Laws passed, thousands of Jewish government workers lost their jobs, along with doctors, lawyers, teachers, professors, performers, journalists, and newspaper editors. Jews who had converted to Christian religions were removed from Church-related positions. In March, Jewish doctors

----
This sign, posted on the door of a German restaurant in 1935, reads "Jews not wanted!"

were no longer allowed to practice in government-run institutions—which included all German hospitals. Jews were banned from using medical facilities operated by non-Jews.

Many Jewish businesses were losing customers. The government shut down others by refusing to renew their operating licenses. Singling out foreign-born Jews for special punishment, the government first revoked the licenses of Jews who had moved to Germany from Poland, followed by others. A few Jews were able to work in secret, however, sometimes aided by non-Jewish friends.

As Jews lost their jobs and businesses, poverty became widespread. The unemployment rate among Jews reached a historical high of 10 percent. Jewish relief organizations struggled to help increasing numbers of people with ever-dwindling resources. Their work was made more difficult because the Jews who stayed in Germany tended to be poorer people and the elderly; the young and the affluent were the most likely to emigrate.

In March, Hitler ordered his troops to invade the Rhineland, a demilitarized region between Germany and France. It was a swift and bloodless military success, delighting Hitler's supporters.

All voters were ordered to take part in an election held at the end of March. Nazi candidates ran unopposed, and there were rumors of harassment and false reporting at the polls. Few were surprised when Hitler claimed 98 percent of the vote.

Classroom Injustices

As Hitler's supporters praised his latest triumph, Jews continued to suffer. Jewish children were often ostracized at school—shunned by classmates, even former friends, and excluded from school and athletic activities. The simple act of buying pencils could require entering a store that displayed demeaning antisemitic posters. Antisemitic teachers gave Jewish students low marks for good work; they ignored those who tried to answer questions, but then penalized them for failing to participate.

Many young people were assaulted after school, often by gangs who belonged to the Hitler Youth. Jewish students often

Hitler's First Defiance

In early 1936, Adolf Hitler ordered his troops into the Rhineland, a region between Germany and France that was demilitarized after World War I. The 1919 Treaty of Versailles had specifically stated that no German troops were allowed in this region. France had demanded that this "buffer zone" be established between the two nations in order to prevent another German invasion.

Around dawn on March 7, German troops—first on motorcycles, then on foot—crossed the bridges that spanned the River Rhine and moved into the Rhineland. Immediately, they set up military posts in the region, a gross violation of international law. For several months, the Germans had been building secret barracks and new roads and rail lines there.

Hitler addressed the members of the Reichstag (Parliament) that day. Greeted by a roaring ovation, he told his fellow parliamentarians:

In the interest of a people's most basic right to secure its borders and preserve its ability for self-defense, the German government has today onward restored unlimited sovereignty in the demilitarized zone of the Rhineland.

He then pledged, "Germany will never break the peace." Years later, people would learn that Hitler had told his troops to withdraw at once without fighting if they met any resistance from French or British troops. Both of those armies were better equipped and trained than the Germans. But neither country risked opposing Germany. Instead, they followed a policy called "Appeasement," meeting Hitler's demands in order to avoid war.

arrived home bruised and bleeding. Walter Weglun, a Jewish boy who attended school in Germany during the 1930s, later recalled, "I . . . had packs [of children] follow me. Not all the time, but sometimes, and I would get beaten up." One day, Weglun's teacher came to school wearing a Nazi uniform. As the only Jewish child in his class, Weglun was forced to sing a popular Nazi song alone.

Because of their long tradition of cherishing education, Jewish parents removed their children from school only as a last resort. By 1936, Jews were running their own schools, where children could continue to learn without being harassed or physically attacked. Funds were scarce, but volunteers worked to run the schools. Jewish professors and schoolteachers who had lost their jobs provided excellent instruction. For funding, these schools relied on contributions and on donations from organizations in the United States and other countries.

Jewish schools became a haven. A student at the Berlin Hochschule, where higher education and rabbinical training were offered, later said, "One could forget the world outside the classroom, the world of . . . inspired hatred which slowly moved toward unspeakable actions of brutality and crime."

The Circle Widens

Hatred of Jews was now being displayed in more places around the world. Individuals who approved of the Nazis' aims seized the opportunity to imitate them. People in countries such as Poland, Austria, and Romania that had already been fostering a deep-rooted antisemitism now expressed it more openly. In the United States, the German-American Bund, Silver Shirts, and Christian Front groups published materials praising Hitler and addressed their followers over the radio.

Hitler reviews 35,000 Nazi troops that assembled in Berlin on February 20, 1936, to celebrate the third anniversary of his chancellorship.

New anti-Jewish laws were passed throughout Europe. Hungary passed laws that deprived Jews of certain jobs, civil rights, and homes and other property. Jewish children there were subjected to name-calling and other humiliations. They were attacked by gangs of youth on the playground and while walking to and from school. Cecilia Bernstein, who was then a child living in a small town in Hungary, said that even policemen beat Jews.

Violence against Jews and their property increased. Anti-Jewish riots took place in Romania, where, as in Germany, Jews were barred from colleges. Jews were subjected to special taxes, and people were urged to boycott

Violence in Poland

Religious prejudice against Jews had ancient roots in Poland. Yet, despite hostile conditions, in 1936, Poland was home to 3.3 million Jews. Through the generations, Polish Jews had built vibrant communities and some of the finest schools and synagogues in Europe. They tended, however, to live apart from other Poles, without inter-marrying. Many only spoke Yiddish rather than Polish.

During the 1930s, anti-Jewish feelings in Poland intensified and spread. Like the Nazis, the Polish government used Jews as scapegoats; it blamed Jews for the country's problems, especially economic hardships.

Violence against Polish Jews occurred regularly. Groups of people attacked Jewish communities with clubs and rocks. Men, women, and children were beaten, and some people were tortured to death. Jewish students were attacked; some were slashed across the face with razor blades.

By the end of 1936, 79 Polish Jews had been killed and approximately 500 injured during more than 350 attacks. With violence steadily on the rise, more than 11,500 Polish Jews left for Palestine. By the end of 1937, approximately 400,000 Polish Jews had emigrated. But millions still remained to face the worst years of the Holocaust.

Jewish businesses. In one episode, two Jews in Timisoara, Romania, were killed when members of the antisemitic Iron Guard political group threw a bomb into a Jewish theater. Rioters in Bucharest and other Romanian communities destroyed Jewish property. In Lithuania, a new law barred Jewish physicians from the university medical faculty.

As the circle of persecution widened, Jews grew more troubled and frustrated. What had they done to be treated so cruelly?

Stefan Lux, one of 2,000 German Jewish film producers who had been ousted from his profession, desperately wanted to show the world what was happening in Europe. On July 3, 1936, the 48-year-old Lux committed suicide in the assembly room of the League of Nations (later the United Nations) building in Geneva, Switzerland. He left behind a letter for British cabinet minister Anthony Eden. In it, Lux spoke movingly of "inhuman indifferences" in the face of Nazi persecution. Lux expressed the hope that his death would "reach the hearts of men."

"Height of Shame"

Adolf Hitler eagerly anticipated the 1936 Summer Olympics in Berlin, where athletes from 52 nations would gather. He believed that these, the 11th modern Olympic Games, would showcase his "superior" Aryan athletes. Hitler played a personal role in planning the Games, ordering that they must be magnificent in every way. He helped to design an elaborate stone stadium that provided seating for 110,000 spectators. A new open-air pool area had seats for 18,000. Trees were dug up from around Berlin, then replanted in a park near the Olympic site.

Hitler hoped to impress visitors who would be flocking to Germany from around the world, especially journalists. Nazi leaders agreed that they would refrain from openly persecuting Jews while foreigners were attending the Olympic Games in Berlin.

Hitler acknowledges the crowd at the Berlin Olympics from his special box at the stadium.

Antisemitic signs, posters, and billboards were pulled down. The crudest antisemitic newspapers, such as *Der Stürmer*, were kept off newsstands.

Many visitors to Germany were fooled by the Nazis' deceptions. They concluded that the stories they had heard about the Nazis must not be true. Visitors praised the clean, crime-free streets, the rise in employment, the new highways, and the happy-looking Germans.

Jewish Athletes on the Sidelines

The United States and other nations had debated whether or not to take part in the Berlin Olympics. In 1934, the American Olympic Committee (AOC) insisted that Germany permit qualified athletes to compete, regardless of their religion. Controversy over the Olympics continued into 1936, as various countries complained that Germany mistreated Jewish athletes and excluded them from its teams.

Between 1933 and 1936, the Nazis banned Jews from sports organizations and competitions and from such jobs as lifeguards and coaches. Margarethe (Gretel) Bergmann, a champion high-jumper, was among those who suffered from this discrimination. In 1933, as she was about to enter the university in Berlin to study physical education, Bergmann was told that she could not attend. She was also expelled from the Ulm Soccer Club, despite her outstanding playing record. Her family moved to England, where she enrolled in school and won the women's British high-jump title in 1934. But Nazi officials ordered her back to Germany to try out for its Olympic team, although she had hoped to compete for Great Britain.

In June of that year, the United States threatened to boycott the Games because no Jews were on the German team. Germany then announced that 21 Jews were training for the Olympics at athletic camps. Bergmann was among them. (She later said that it was ironic to be considered for the German Olympic team at the same time that Jews were being banned from recreational facilities, restaurants, movies, and concerts.) But, though Bergmann attended training sessions, she was not allowed to compete with non-Jews.

By the fall of 1935, the AOC still had not decided if the United States would compete in Berlin. German officials hastily added Bergmann and fencing champion Helene Mayer, who had a Jewish father and a Christian mother, to their team. Mayer had won a first-place gold medal at the 1928 Olympics and a second-place silver in the 1932 Olympics, in Los Angeles.

On June 30, Gretel Bergmann matched the high-jump record for German women. Yet, in July, she was told that she had not made the German team. After years of preparation for the Olympics, Bergmann was forced to the sidelines. In 1938, after becoming an American citizen, Bergmann won the U.S. women's high-jump title. In 1980, she was inducted into the Jewish Sports Hall of Fame in Israel.

The American Superstar

The Berlin Olympics began on August 1, 1936. Thousands of Germans of all ages marched and played musical instruments in official Olympic ceremonies and parades. Singers and dancers performed elaborate routines. Among the participants were 28,000 members of various Hitler youth groups.

Hitler appeared in full military dress for the dramatic opening ceremonies. His shiny limousine had traveled down Berlin's swastika-draped streets before purposely arriving at the same time as the Olympic torch. He was greeted with loud cheers from masses of spectators as he took the seat of honor at the stadium. Author Thomas Wolfe later described Hitler as "a little dark man with a comic-opera mustache, erect and standing, moveless and unsmiling, with his hand upraised, palm outward...."

The Olympic athletes represented many nationalities and religions, including those that the Nazis considered "inferior." There were blacks, Asians, Arabs, Hispanics, and people of mixed heritage. Hitler felt sure that his "Aryan" athletes, whom he viewed as "racially pure superhumans," could defeat all others.

Hitler's plan was not realized. Two African Americans, Cornelius Johnson and David Albritten, won first and second place in the high jump. Kitei Son of Korea won the marathon race, while Japanese athletes dominated swimming and diving events. Ibola Czak, a Hungarian Jew, won the women's high jump. Many other "non-Aryans" also won medals.

Germany's best male runner, Erich Borchmeyer, was outclassed by an African American, Jesse Owens, a student at Ohio State University. Owens won the first of four gold medals in the 100-meter dash in world-record time: 10.3 seconds. When an aide to Hitler suggested that he invite Owens to his box, Hitler replied, "Do you really think that I will allow myself to be photographed shaking hands with a Negro?"

Awed by Owens's amazing speed, German spectators cheered, and children sought his autograph. His friendliness and good manners made Owens popular with fans. Max Von Der Grun recalled that, after the Olympics, "We used to play at being Jesse Owens; whoever could jump the farthest or run the fastest or throw some object the greatest distance became Jesse Owens." The teachers forbade these games. But they had no good answer when the children asked how a person from an "inferior" race could be so accomplished.

Olympic runners Marty Glickman and Sam Stoller—both Jews—were slated to run the 400-meter (1,312-foot) relay for the U.S. team. At the last minute, however, the coaches substituted Jesse Owens and Ralph Metcalfe for Glickman and Stoller. A number of excuses were given at the time, but it wasn't until later that the motivations of the coaches were more closely examined. Avery Brundage, the powerful president of the American Olympic Committee, had firmly supported the coaches' decision. He also belonged to a number of antisemitic U.S. organizations, most notably America First and the German-American Bund. As facts came out, it seemed that Glickman and Stoller had been prohibited from competing because they were Jews, and with Avery Brundage's full complicity.

The Games, designed to promote fellowship and goodwill, would become another casualty of the Nazis. There would be no Olympics in 1940 or in 1944. Among the many victims of the Holocaust would be Jewish athletes Alfred and Gustav Flatow, winners of Olympic gold medals in gymnastics in 1896. Captain Wolfgang Furstner, the director of the Olympic Village at the 1936 Games in Berlin, would later commit suicide in the face of Nazi persecution.

The minority of non-Jewish Germans who opposed the Nazis dreaded Hitler's next move. In August 1936, Friedrich Percyval Reck-Malleczewen, a former government official and member of a prominent German family, wrote:

I wrack my brains over the perpetual riddle of how this same people which so jealously watched over its rights a few years ago can have sunk into this stupor. . . dominated by the street-corner idlers of yesterday. . . .

Reck-Malleczewen said it was the "height of shame" that his homeland was "incapable any longer of perceiving its shame for the shame that it is." To Reck-Malleczewen, Adolf Hitler was "no human being." He believed that Hitler was full of self-hatred and vanity and that these traits would lead Germany's leader to "set fire to the world."

Gold medalist Jesse Owens salutes as others "Heil Hitler" during award ceremonies at the Berlin Olympics.

"It Won't Happen Here"

While showing a friendly face to the world during the Olympic Games in Berlin, Adolf Hitler was secretly making plans to attack neighboring countries. When a bloody civil war broke out in Spain in 1936, Hitler quickly supported Spain's Fascist leader, General Francisco Franco. Germany sent supplies and soldiers to help Franco's troops overthrow the Spanish Republic and set up a right-wing dictatorship. Hitler also strengthened his ties with Fascist Italy, under its premier–dictator, Benito Mussolini. Mussolini had recently led an Italian invasion of Ethiopia and was also giving Franco his support.

Trouble for Italian Jews

In November 1936, Hitler and Mussolini formed the Rome–Berlin Axis, which made allies of their two nations. Needless to say, Italian Jews became alarmed. In the past, they had felt reassured

----
The contents of a synagogue in Trieste, Italy, in ruins after an outbreak of antisemitic violence.

when Mussolini criticized Hitler. In 1934, Hitler had become angry at some former supporters and ordered approximately 200 people to be murdered, in what became known as the "Night of the Long Knives." Mussolini then criticized the German leader, saying, "It would mean the end of European civilization if this country of murderers...were to overrun Europe."

Mussolini had often said that the Nazi government differed from his own, saying:

> . . .fascism is a regime that is rooted in the great cultural traditions of the Italian people; fascism recognizes the right of the individual, it recognizes religion and family. National Socialism [Nazism], on the other hand, is savage barbarism.

To Nahum Goldmann, a leader in the World Jewish Congress, Mussolini remarked, "[Hitler] is an idiot, a rascal, a fanatical rascal, an insufferable talker. It is a torture to listen to him."

Italy had a long tradition of religious tolerance, and Italian Jews and Christians had built lasting social and business ties. Many Jews had supported Mussolini. Yet some worried after Mussolini invaded Ethiopia that year, angering Great Britain, France, and other nations. This aggressive act brought Italy closer to Germany. However, when antisemitic articles appeared in some Italian newspapers in 1935, Italian leaders did not support them. When Jews were criticized for attending meetings of international Jewish groups, Italy's Minister of the Interior pointed out that this gave Italian Jews a chance to improve public relations.

By 1936, antisemitism in Italy seemed to be rising. *The Jews in Italy*, a critical book by Paolo Orano, was used to attack Jews. Orano said that Jews as a group were a subversive influence wherever they settled and that they tended to view themselves as superior. Yet Orano had several close Jewish friends. One of them, Ettore Ovazza, lived in Turin. He was a respected attorney, a war veteran, and a Jewish community leader. He was also an important member of Italy's Fascist Party.

In 1937, Franca Ovazza, Ettore's teenage daughter, was arrested and beaten by members of the Italian secret police. She had begun criticizing the government after returning home from attending a Swiss school. Franca later recalled:

I was very proud of being from Italy, this great country that had become even greater with the African war [in Ethiopia]. And in Switzerland, I suddenly realized this was not how the world saw it. Other people had freedom, they weren't grouped in uniforms. They saw Mussolini not as a great man but as an oppressor.

The next summer, Ovazza heard a list of new anti-Jewish laws broadcast over the Italian radio, including a law that banned Jewish children from attending school. She said, "We started crying and crying. That was the end of our world…all our friends would be going on to university and we would be left outside."

Pressured by right-wing political groups—and wanting to cement his alliance with the now-powerful Germany, Mussolini had yielded to Hitler's continuing demands that Italy pass anti-Jewish measures. The Italian government, however, made certain exceptions. It excluded from restrictions any Jews who had been wounded or awarded medals in World War I and those who had been quick to join the Fascist Party. Those who were not in these categories, however, could not join the party, hold public jobs, own large businesses or tracts of land, or marry non-Jews.

More racial laws in Italy were passed in 1937 and 1938, and no one was exempted, not even those defined earlier as "patriotic Fascist Jews." All Jews were expelled from the Fascist Party, the armed forces, public jobs, businesses with more than 100 employees, banks, and national-defense businesses. Jews could not hire non-Jewish domestic workers. Within another year, Jewish doctors, lawyers, architects, journalists, dentists, engineers, and accountants were barred from their professions.

Franca Ovazza recalled, "My father was not able to work. My sister and I were not able to go to school. Those things were shattering to us." Although some non-Jews shunned them, Ovazza said, "Most of our friends were marvelous." Just as had happened in Germany, Italian Jews started their own schools, often staffed by those who had been forced out of the universities.

To avoid persecution, about 5,700 Italian Jews converted to Catholicism; many others were given fake baptismal certificates by sympathetic priests. Some Jews, desperate and without hope, killed themselves. Others fled to South America, Cuba, Switzerland, and the United States.

One of these refugees was Enrico Fermi, a world-famous physicist who left because his wife, Laura, was Jewish. Fermi decided to leave Europe in 1938, after hearing that he had won the Nobel Prize. After the award ceremony in Sweden, Enrico, Laura, and their two children boarded a ship for the United States. There, Fermi became a professor at Columbia University and continued his ground-breaking research in nuclear physics.

Together with other brilliant scientists, many of them also refugees from Europe, Fermi worked on the Manhattan Project during World War II. The U.S. government financed this project to build the world's first atomic bomb. Upon hearing rumors that Nazi Germany was also working on such a bomb, the United States had organized and funded the project to keep Hitler from being the first to harness atomic energy.

"Aryanization"

During 1937, Hitler speeded up a process that he termed the "Aryanization" of the German economy. He planned to transfer all assets and complete control of German businesses to those Germans he called Aryans. As part of this plan, the Nazi government began seizing all remaining Jewish-owned property. Jewish business owners received letters from the government telling them that their establishments were now illegal and must be shut down. They had no choice but to sell for whatever price they could get, usually much less than true value. Many buyers took advantage of this opportunity to profit at the expense of others.

On April 26, Jews were ordered to register all their property with the government. Nazi officials used this information to carry out their plan to take everything the Jews owned. In July, Jews were banned from working as office managers, tour guides, and real estate agents or brokers. With each passing month, more German Jews slid into poverty.

Yet, for other Germans, jobs were more plentiful. A new law required all men at the age of 18 to serve for at least two years in the armed forces. As more men entered the military, many German factories did not have enough workers. To fill the gap, women were allowed to work in factories; only a few years before, they had been confined to childrearing and housework. Some Germans worried that the military buildup and arms production meant that Hitler planned to start a war. He assured them that these measures were for defense, in case France or Great Britain attacked Germany. Nazi propaganda frequently warned of possible attacks from these countries, and many Germans believed it.

Factory jobs, like others, were closed to Jews. In just two years, many families had lost their money, homes, and other possessions. People also suffered from the stress of losing their identity as workers and professionals and their status in society. The injustice of the losses made these hardships all the more bitter. And even more ominous were the stories of those who had been arrested and who were sent to Nazi concentration camps.

Horrifying Stories

In 1937, thousands of people were arrested and sent to concentration camps. About 96 percent of these prisoners were Jewish. Many of the others were political prisoners—people who had spoken out against the Nazis or broken rules, such as listening to a foreign radio station or reading a banned book or newspaper.

Concentration camp prisoners were treated brutally by their captors. Many were forced into hard labor; for example, working long hours in stone quarries. To destroy them physically, Nazis *physical* beat prisoners and deprived them of food, water, and medical care. Many starved to death. Constant verbal abuse and humiliation aimed at breaking their spirit.

Some desperate prisoners committed suicide; some were shot while trying to escape. People might also be shot for breaking minor rules, such as walking too near a guard. After killing a prisoner, Nazi guards often made it look as though the person had tried to escape.

The Suffering of Non-Jews

In July 1937, a new concentration camp opened in Buchenwald, Germany. One of the first arrivals was a Protestant minister named Paul Schneider. He had been arrested several times for giving anti-Nazi sermons and refusing to salute the Nazi flag. Pastor Schneider died at Buchenwald two years later, after being subjected to repeated, savage beatings.

A man who was later released from Buchenwald described the horrors he had witnessed there, calling it the "City of Sorrow." Photographs taken during those years at Buchenwald show emaciated, sickly prisoners. People were forced to stand for hours in all kinds of weather during daily roll-calls without adequate food or clothing. Those who fell or fainted were beaten. Guards tortured people in various ways; some, for example, were hung up by their arms.

Others at Buchenwald included members of the Jehovah's Witnesses Church. These inmates were identified by the brown triangles that were sewn on their clothing. As pacifists—people who oppose war—Jehovah's Witnesses refused to serve in the army. Nor would they give the Nazi salute, since their faith required them to pledge allegiance only to God. During the Nazi regime, nearly 6,000 Witnesses were arrested and more than 2,000 died in concentration camps.

Baron von Lessner, head of the Catholic Schools Association, was a non-Jewish captive at the notorious German concentration camp Dachau. He was murdered there, as was Richard Schmitz,

A line-up of Romani prisoners during roll-call at Dachau.

the former mayor of Vienna, Austria, whose political views also led to his arrest. The Nazis further offended the grief-stricken families of those who died by demanding a payment in exchange for each victim's ashes.

Many Romani were also imprisoned. A large group of Romani living in Germany had been arrested in July of 1936 and sent to Dachau. The Nazis singled out the Romani, along with Jews, for destruction. At least 200,000 Romani would die during the Holocaust.

In the years to come, as the Nazis invaded other lands, they would fill the camps with more victims—resistance workers, people who helped Jews, male homosexuals, political dissidents. Many of them would suffer and die along with millions of Jewish men, women, and children.

"God Commands Us to Speak"

On July 1, 1937, many people were upset to hear that Pastor Martin Niemöller had been arrested. Niemöller, a highly decorated veteran of World War I, had publicly opposed the Nazis. He helped to found the Confessing Church, an anti-Fascist branch of the Lutheran Church in Germany, made up of both clergy and lay people. He also organized the Pastors Emergency League, which numbered several thousand members.

In his writings and sermons, Niemöller objected to government interference with the churches and to the Nazis' treatment of Jews. He warned that the Nazis would destroy Christianity, since its values clashed with their ideology. In Berlin, Niemöller declared, "No more will we keep silent; God commands us to speak. One must obey God rather than man."

After his arrest, Niemöller was put on trial, which most acknowledged to be a sham. He was then sentenced for an indefinite amount of time to the Sachsenhausen concentration camp. The charges classified him as an "anti-social parasite." The following Sunday, Protestant ministers throughout Germany read a statement expressing their deep concern. The Nazis completely ignored them.

Niemöller was sometimes confined to the notorious bunker section of the camps. There, solitary prisoners were forced to stand day and night in an unlit, narrow space. Many people died in these bunkers during the war. Niemöller, however, somehow managed to survive his eight-year imprisonment. He remained in various Nazi camps until he was freed by Allied troops in 1945.

Trapped

German Jews were being told they were unwanted in their homeland—but, at the same time, the Nazis now made it very difficult for Jews to leave the country. Elaborate procedures required numerous papers to be filled out and carried from one government office to another.

Guards were even dispatched to watch as Jews packed their personal belongings, in order to make sure that they followed strict rules about what could be taken abroad. For example, Jews were limited to taking only $10 in cash—obviously, nowhere near enough to start a new life.

Many of the Jews who found refuge in other European countries would later be caught in the ever-widening Nazi net. Among them was the family of Otto Frank, whose daughter Anne was to write a diary that would become known throughout the world. The Frank family fled Germany in 1933, but the Nazis later tormented them again after Germany invaded Holland in 1940.

In 1932, Sholom Heller moved his family from Romania to Antwerp, Belgium, after he was beaten by anti-Jewish thugs on his way to vote in an election. He began a soda-bottling business. His four children—Frieda, Clara, Elie, and Heshie—attended school, made new friends, and felt safe.

Early in 1938, when his brother Emil urged him to leave Europe completely, Sholom said, "World opinion will stop Hitler. And we can't run again. Once is enough." His wife commented, "It won't happen here."

But world opinion did not stop Hitler. Not one prominent world leader firmly confronted the Nazis during those years. The Heller family watched in horror as Hitler's troops entered and took military control of Sudetenland, a region of Czechoslovakia, in 1938. Belgium would be invaded by Nazi troops in May 1940, followed by anti-Jewish laws, restrictions, propaganda, and pogroms. Deportations to death camps followed soon after. Like so many others, the Heller family—who believed they had found safety—would be trapped once again.

"Marching Boots Everywhere"

By 1938, Adolf Hitler had ruled Germany for five years. Hundreds of Jews and political opponents had been killed; tens of thousands of others had fled. As the Nazis stepped up their police activity, life became even more difficult for Germany's remaining Jews. On February 10, 1938, the German police and Gestapo were united and fell under the direction of the larger SS. This became the supreme police agency in the land, empowered to arrest anyone it saw fit. The future looked ominous. Some people guessed that Hitler was heading toward war. The *Führer* had often spoken about his wish that Austria, the land of his birth, join his expanding empire. Early in 1938, he made that wish a reality.

"Homecoming into the Reich"

On March 13, 1938, Hitler declared that Austria was a part of his Third Reich. During a private meeting the day before, he had threatened Austrian chancellor Kurt von Schuschnigg until he finally

----
Austrians welcome the arrival of Hitler and the Nazis in 1938 with a Nazi salute and a sign that reads "The workers of Vienna thank the Führer."

agreed to turn over his government to the Nazis. German troops marched unopposed into Austria. The annexation (joining) of that country to Germany came to be known as the *Anschluss*. Although some people—including some Christians, the Socialists, and the Austrian Jews—dreaded this event, most Austrians seemed pleased. People cheered and gave the Nazi salute, and many hung Nazi flags on their homes. Signs proclaimed that day as the "Homecoming into the Reich," and a popular slogan became "One People, One Country, One *Führer.*"

Nazi Party members proudly displayed their swastika armbands, which had been forbidden during the years that Chancellor Schuschnigg led Austria. Ultimately, a higher percentage of Austrians would join the Nazi Party than did Germans. Fully 75 percent of the guards in the concentration camps would be Austrians, as would most of the troops in charge of transporting Jews to death camps.

Hitler lied about the reason for his Austrian invasion, telling people that his troops had marched into Austria to keep order and prevent riots. In secret, he had Nazi police put Schuschnigg under house arrest. The former chancellor endured months of abuse at the hands of the Nazis.

The Nazis then arranged an election so that Austrians could "vote" on the takeover. Ballots featured a large circle that people could mark *Ja* ("Yes") and a much smaller one for *Nein* ("No"). The vote was overwhelmingly in favor of what Hitler called "the reunion of Austria with the German Reich." Rumors spread throughout Germany that the election was not run honestly. A number of Germans had voted "No" and knew others who had done the same. Yet polls in various towns announced that every voter had marked "Yes."

"Sadistic" Persecution

About 183,000 Jews lived in Austria. Most lived in Vienna, the capital, where they made up one-sixth of the population. After setting up a police state in Austria, the Nazis began persecuting

Austrian Jews. Hitler immediately imposed anti-Jewish laws like those in Germany. Austrian Jews were no longer citizens; they lost all their rights. They could not use restaurants, public parks, or swimming pools. All Jewish businesses and offices were labeled with a red *J*, and Nazi police harassed and arrested non-Jews who attempted to enter.

boycott

American journalist William Shirer described the persecution of Austrian Jews as "sadistic," even worse than what he had seen in Germany. Austrian Jews were attacked and robbed on the streets.

The Haganah

As Jews in Europe found themselves increasingly trapped and persecuted, certain Jewish organizations tried to help. Secret groups sprang up to hide people and help them find ways to escape danger. An underground defense group from Palestine, the Haganah, operated a number of farms in the Austrian countryside. There, young people were protected from the violence and threats of Viennese streets and were trained in survival skills they might need while on the run. Refugees were also taught farming and trades so that they could find work more easily after they emigrated.

When efforts at legal emigration failed, desperate people turned to illegal means. Using its connections abroad, Haganah was able to help hundreds of people leave by ship. The group gave these refugees false identification papers and visas in order to get them to Palestine and elsewhere.

Ehud Avriel, an Austrian-born Jew who turned 21 in 1938, was among those who worked with Haganah. Among the different people who assisted his group were a Hungarian-born restaurant owner named Pataki, a high-ranking Austrian Nazi official named Wolfgang Karthaus, a wealthy Italian, and Gerta Haas, a Jewish woman married to an Austrian nobleman.

Avriel and his colleagues in Haganah worked underground throughout the war, facing great danger in order to rescue Jews from the Nazis. Although he could have remained safely in Palestine, Avriel returned by parachute into Nazi-occupied territory on many occasions. He operated by delivering messages, money, and other things to the resistance and helping people to escape. He was one of many brave Jewish men and women who resisted the Nazis and tried to help a struggling people survive a devastating era.

Hundreds of people, young and old, were stopped at random by Nazis and humiliated. One witness, Erika Weihs, recalled:

I heard marching boots everywhere. It seemed everyone had his radio on. I heard Hitler's voice from every window. I saw a girl I knew on her knees, cleaning the street with a brush. A few SS men were standing over her.

Witnesses reported that the police enjoyed finding new ways to degrade people, such as making them crawl on the ground and eat grass. One Jewish man was forced to wash the pavement with a bucket of water that had been mixed with acid. The Nazis singled out well-educated, professional people—they seemed to particularly resent those who had been successful. Hundreds of elderly people died of heart attacks while being abused.

Thea Sonnenmark, a child in Vienna at that time, recalled:

At the end of March 1938, as my father went to open his grocery store, the SA [Nazi stormtroopers] gave him a toothbrush and ordered him to scrub the street. Some of his non-Jewish customers came by, and when they saw my father there, they laughed and jeered. These were customers of long standing. He considered them to be his friends.

News of the *Anschluss* reached other countries. In Amsterdam, Holland, a young woman named Miep Gies worked at a food-products company owned by a German Jewish refugee, Otto Frank. She later recalled a day in March 1938, when all of the employees stood together listening to Mr. Frank's radio. They stood silent as a dramatic voice announced Hitler's triumphal entry into the city of his youth, Vienna. The radio announcer described the atmosphere of flowers and flags and cheering, euphoric crowds. "All of us were soon stunned when the news came that Viennese Jews had been made to clean out public toilets and to scrub the streets in an orgy of Nazi depravity."

For Austrian Jews, life became increasingly miserable. Austrians in hundreds of villages and towns throughout the country hastened to drive out Jews, some of them from families that had lived there for generations. Menacing gangs visited homes and warned people to leave. Jewish shop owners found ugly signs and pictures scrawled on their windows. Non-Jews were taken to police headquarters and told to break off all business and social relationships with Jews.

When rules and insults failed, the Nazis used physical force to drive Jews out of Austria. One Sunday night, 51 Jews were taken from their homes in Burgenland. All of their possessions were stolen. They were loaded onto boats,

Celebrants from Vienna welcome the arrival of German troops with a sign that reads "Sieg Heil [salute] to the Führer."

then pushed into the Danube River, where they were stranded until the Czechoslovakian government on the other side allowed them to enter.

June 1938 brought mass arrests in Vienna. More than 2,000 Jews were detained or picked up at random, on any pretext. Some, for example, were arrested for jaywalking or for a minor traffic violation. For this, they were sent to the concentration camps at Dachau and Buchenwald. Jews were not safe anywhere, particularly not on the streets of Vienna. Many fled to the countryside.

In desperation, some Austrian Jews killed themselves. Among these victims were prominent authors, historians, scientists, and legal scholars. G.E.R. Gedye, a British journalist who lived in Vienna, observed some Nazis reading with obvious pleasure lists of people who had been driven to suicide.

------------ The Evian Conference: "Slammed Doors" ------------

In 1938, U.S. president Franklin Roosevelt called for an international conference to discuss issues surrounding Jewish refugees. The conference was held at Evian, a French resort town, from July 5 to 15. Thirty-two countries—the United States, Canada, Great Britain, France, Belgium, Switzerland, Norway, Denmark, Holland, New Zealand, Australia, South Africa, and 20 Latin American republics—sent representatives. Attendees heard speakers from more than 40 organizations. But critics noted that some groups, including the World Jewish Congress—which represented some 7 million Jews—had only a few minutes to speak. Others did not get to speak at all.

Most countries refused to accept more Jewish refugees, citing the over-population and unemployment that stemmed from the Great Depression.

The Hotel Royal in Evian, France, hosted the 1938 international conference.

Some nations, including Canada, Colombia, Uruguay, and Venezuela, argued that they needed only agricultural workers. Peru and some others objected to admitting more professional people, as that might upset the politically powerful upper classes in these countries. Some nations said that they would exclude people who were "traders and intellectuals." A representative from Australia used the false concept of "race" as an excuse for not accepting Jews. He said, "As we have no real racial problem we are not desirous of importing one." New Zealand also did not lift or amend its immigration restrictions.

Argentina, Chile, Uruguay, and Mexico set strict limits on Jewish immigration—in Mexico, for example, just 100 people a year. The United States agreed to take only its previously set

In Germany, Friedrich Percyval Reck-Malleczewen continued to denounce the actions of his countrymen. In his diary, he wrote that the German troops had lost all sense of honor and no longer understood "that boundaries exist between right and wrong. . . ." For his outspokenness, he was arrested in 1944 and sent to Dachau, where he died the next spring.

quota of 27,370 German and Austrian immigrants. This was but a small proportion of those desperately seeking to escape the Nazis.

The Dominican Republic in the Caribbean was a remarkable exception. It offered to take 100,000 refugees. Holland and Denmark, long known for humanitarian ideals, also promised to take more people. By 1938, some 25,000 Jews had escaped to Holland, a small country. Although it was already densely populated, Denmark agreed to take as many refugees as possible.

A committee was set up to continue studying the matter, but no real actions were taken. On July 8, the *New York Herald Tribune* summed it up with its headline: "Powers Slam Doors Against German Jews."

An unanticipated but tragic effect of the Evian Conference was that it actually aided Nazi propaganda. The Nazis' publications boasted that few nations were willing to accept large numbers of Jewish immigrants. Some historians have said that Nazi leaders interpreted the dispassionate response from other countries as an unspoken "approval," a

U.S. representative Myron Taylor addresses attendees at the Evian Conference.

signal that they need not temper their actions against Jews.

Among those present at Evian was Golda Myerson, an eloquent woman who would later be known as Golda Meir, a prime minister of Israel. Myerson had left New York City to help build the Jewish homeland in Palestine. During an interview with reporters after the Evian Conference, she said, "There is one ideal I have in mind, one thing I want to see before I die—that my people should not need expressions of sympathy any more."

In August 1938, SS officer Adolf Eichmann became the head of the immigration office for Jews in Vienna. There, he set up the Office of Jewish Emigration, which aimed to force as many Jews as possible out of the Third Reich. In the years that followed, during World War II, Eichmann would send millions to die in concentration camps.

Fleeing from the Reich

More than 98,000 Jews, about half of the total in Austria, fled in terror. By mid-1938, more than 150,000 German and Austrian Jews had settled elsewhere. For example, many went to the United States (approximately 55,000), Palestine (40,000), Great Britain (8,000), France (15,000), Switzerland (more than 14,000), Brazil (8,000), Bolivia (several thousand), Belgium (2,000), Sweden (1,000), Denmark (845), and Norway (150).

Synagogues in Flames

By 1938, the Nazis had expanded the boundaries of persecution to include the defacing and destruction of Jewish houses of worship. These acts were especially painful to Jews, as their synagogues were not only places for religious services but were also centers of community life. They were centers for educational programs as well as activities for young people. They also held an array of sacred objects—some of which had been handed down for centuries—that were vital to Jewish religious ceremonies.

In June, the Jews of Munich could only watch as their old and beautiful synagogue was set on fire. That same month, the Jewish congregation of Nuremberg was informed by Nazi officials that their synagogue and the attached buildings must be demolished. After meeting with the congregation, the Jewish leaders decided not to give their consent. In response, on August 3, the Nuremberg Town Council declared that it would dispossess the congregation of its buildings. The officials based their actions on a 1937 law that authorized the renovation of German cities and on a 1938 decree that specified what kinds of buildings could be located in cities where Nazi Party conferences were held. Nuremberg was the site of large Nazi Party rallies as well as the place where the Nazi Parliament held its meetings. Jewish leaders were warned of the upcoming demolition and had barely enough time to remove the Holy Scrolls and other sacred objects that were housed there.

Julius Streicher, a zealous Nazi leader and propagandist, turned the demolition of the Nuremberg synagogue into an elaborate spectacle. As part of his show, he invited important Nazi officials to watch the destruction. On August 10, as a crowd gathered, Streicher himself removed the large Star of David from the synagogue. Minutes later, Nazis dynamited the walls and pillars.

A Sudeten woman weeps as she salutes Hitler at a procession in the fall of 1938.

Thousands more Jews wanted to emigrate. They lined up during the night at the U.S. and British embassies in order to get their names on emigration lists. A few people escaped without visas—legal permits—to enter other countries.

Neighboring countries often refused to admit Jews. Great Britain limited the number of visas it would issue for people to enter Palestine, ignoring the pleas of Jewish organizations around the world. They did this despite the fact that Jews already living in Palestine had declared they would accept responsibility for an unlimited number of Jews escaping persecution in Europe.

That persecution continued to intensify. On August 17, 1938, the Nazi government announced that all Jewish men whose first names were not clearly "Jewish" must add the middle name "Israel." A similar law required Jewish women to use "Sarah," a name from the Hebrew Bible (sometimes called the Old Testament) that had often been given to Jewish girls. In October, the government began stamping the letter *J* on their passports. The Swiss government had asked German authorities to take this step in order to determine who was trying to enter Switzerland.

Fall of the Sudetenland

As the only democracy in Central Europe, Czechoslovakia was known for its fair and tolerant policies. Jews had lived there for hundreds of years and had built vital communities, especially in the western part of the country.

After Hitler rose to power, Czech Jews were harassed by German-speaking Nazis in Sudetenland, the western part of Czechoslovakia along the German border. Sudeten Germans wanted to be united with Germany—something Hitler also desired. Having gained Austria, Hitler was now ready to take over Czechoslovakia. Hitler organized armed troops along the Czech border with Austria. To gain public support, he told people that Sudeten Germans were being mistreated by Czechs. He then demanded control over the Sudetenland.

"Peace for Our Time"

Other nations, including Czechoslovakia's main ally, France, desperately wanted to avoid another major war, especially with the Germans. They urged Czech president Edvard Benes to yield, in the hope that this kind of submission would satisfy Hitler and end Germany's military aggression.

In the interest of appeasement, Great Britain and France signed the Munich Pact, or Munich Agreement, with Germany and Italy on September 29. In this pact, they agreed that Germany could occupy the Sudetenland without interference. British prime minister Neville Chamberlain declared that the Munich Pact would bring "peace for our time."

Italy's Benito Mussolini shakes hands with Great Britain's Prime Minister Neville Chamberlain at the Munich Conference, September 28–29, 1938. Hermann Goering and Hitler (obscured) stand on the left.

Hitler's annexation of Sudetenland was complete on October 1, 1938. For his part, Hitler promised that this was his final territorial claim in Europe. The Czechs, who deeply resented the German occupation, were not given any choice.

As German troops took over the Sudetenland, synagogues were burned down. Jewish homes and businesses were looted. Nearly every Jew in the region, about 20,000, fled. German police arrested the Jews who remained and sent them to concentration camps. Dachau was enlarged, and another camp was built in Flossenburg.

That autumn, long meetings were held by Gestapo leaders, who controlled the police throughout the Third Reich. The concentration camps at Buchenwald and Sachsenhausen were being enlarged, and shipments of clothing for new prisoners began arriving. Prisoners at Dachau were told to sew yellow Stars of David on thousands of striped uniforms. The Nazis were planning a massive attack on Jews throughout "Greater Germany," which now included Germany, Austria, and the Sudetenland.

"Why Are They Beating Us?"

The year 1938 brought intensified levels of violence against Jews throughout Greater Germany. For months, top Nazi officials, particularly the leaders of the Gestapo, had been planning a large-scale, nationwide attack that would terrorize Jews and push more to emigrate. Finally, in November, they saw their chance to carry it out. They knew that Jews had no way to resist; a few weeks earlier, the government had ordered Jews to turn in any and all weapons or else face 20 years in a concentration camp.

Stripped of a Country

According to a 1933 census, more than 56,000 Polish Jews lived in Germany. Some had worked there for 30 years or more. Early in October 1938, they received dreadful news: Polish officials announced that any Jews who had resided outside Poland for five

---

The Fasanenstrasse Synagogue—Berlin's grandest—was one of more than 1,000 synagogues destroyed on the night of November 9, 1938.

or more years would not be eligible for passports. In essence, this made them stateless persons, people without a country.

The German government responded by ordering all Polish-born Jews to leave Germany at once. On October 18, these people were told to pack no more than one suitcase, and then they were taken to railroad stations in Leipzig, Cologne, Dusseldorf, and other towns. By night, they were delivered to the Polish border, where soldiers forced them across at gunpoint. People who did not move quickly enough were whipped.

Thousands of men, women, and children were then trapped in border towns when the Polish government refused to admit them. Tired, hungry, worried, and not knowing their fate, these Jews waited in stables and pigsties.

Among these refugees were Sendel Grynszpan and his family. In Paris, 17-year-old Herschel Grynszpan, Sendel's son, received a disturbing postcard. His father and sister Berta described how they had been forced out of their homes. They were left with many others at Sbnszyn, Poland, in a cold, cramped army camp without enough food.

German Jewish teenager Herschel Grynszpan killed a Nazi official in retaliation for the persecution of Jews, especially members of his family.

Infuriated by the way the German government had treated his family, the teenager bought a gun. On November 7, he entered the German Embassy in Paris, where he managed to make his way to the office of Ernst vom Rath, a low-level official. Grynszpan shot vom Rath, saying that he acted "in the name of twelve thousand persecuted Jews...." After being arrested, Grynszpan told police that the Nazis had chased down his family and treated them like animals. "Being a Jew is not a crime," he said. "I am not a dog. I have a right to live and the Jewish people have a right to exist on this earth."

Vom Rath died two days later. German newspapers declared that the shooting was part of a "world Jewish conspiracy." Nazi leaders now had a convenient excuse to launch a terrifying pogrom they had been planning for many months. It would become known as *Kristallnacht.*

Orders to Destroy

Since they had already planned the main aspects of the pogrom, Nazi leaders were able to act swiftly. They ordered massive attacks on Jewish homes, shops, schools, and other property, to occur overnight on November 9–10. Squads made up of stormtroopers (armed Nazi patrols referred to as "brown-shirts"), Hitler Youth, and other Nazi groups were formed all over Germany. They were given lists of places to destroy and were then supplied with axes, hatchets, picks, and other tools.

Official papers from Gestapo files show that, on November 8, the government sent local police teletyped messages saying that outbreaks of violence would take place throughout Germany and warning, "They are not to be stopped. . . . " In other words, the police were ordered to stand by and let the violence occur.

Giving further instructions, Heinrich Himmler, the head of the Gestapo, said:

> *Preparations are to be made for the arrest of about 20,000–30,000 Jews in the Reich. Wealthy Jews in particular are to be selected. More detailed instructions will be issued in the course of this night.*

Himmler also said that, if any Jews were found to possess weapons, "the most severe measures are to be taken."

Newspaper articles continued to inflame the German public. On November 8, a newspaper declared,

> *We shall no longer tolerate the hundreds of thousands of Jews within our territory who control entire streets of shops, who avail themselves of our public entertainments, and as foreign landlords pocket the wealth of German leaseholders while their brothers in religion incite war on Germany and assassinate German officials.*

"Night of Broken Glass"

Early on the evening of November 9, some 30,000 Nazis gathered at a rally in Nuremberg. They were given hatchets and told they could do whatever they wanted to Jews or their property.

In cities and towns throughout "Greater Germany," gangs arrived in trucks and swept across streets, swinging clubs and smashing windows. They rang doorbells and broke in when nobody answered. Furniture was pulled apart, curtains were slashed, toys and dolls were broken, mirrors and windows were shattered. This was *Kristallnacht*, known as "Night of Broken Glass."

Bernt Engelmann recalled hearing "axe-blows, splintering wood, shrill cries. . . ." Inside the opened door of an apartment of a Jewish family in his apartment building, Engelmann saw glass from a large mirror in the foyer lay in thousands of shards on the floor, and a chest of drawers had been hacked to pieces.

I heard a cupboard full of dishes and glassware fall over with a crash. More axe-blows followed. Bits of wood, feathers from pillows and comforters, and scraps of cloth came flying into the stairwell. . . . I heard a scream, then another—of a child shrieking in terror.

Some German youths of about 17 or 18, Engelmann's age, were stuffing silverware into their pockets and slicing an oil painting on the wall. When Engelmann asked a neighbor to call the police, she shook her head and pointed outside: The police were standing right there. Another man reported seeing a woman and two small children out in the cold with coats over their nightclothes: "They were in a state of terror. 'Why are they beating us?' the woman screamed. 'We haven't done anything!'"

As Jews fled or were chased from their homes, they were harassed and beaten. Jewish men in Baden-Baden were forced to march to the synagogue and to read parts of Hitler's fiercely antisemitic book, *Mein Kampf* ("My Struggle"). Afterwards, the Nazis burned the synagogue.

Desecration

The Nazis destroyed or damaged more than 1,000 synagogues during the night of November 9 and morning of November 10. Virtually all places of worship, large and small, ornate and plain, were ruthlessly vandalized or violated.

The great Berlin Synagogue was among those burned to the ground. A witness, Dr. Benno Cohen, remembered:

Germans in Berlin pass by the shattered shop window of a Jewish-owned business that was destroyed during *Kristallnacht*.

The fire brigade was there, but did not lift a finger. They were instructed to be on the spot only for the protection of the nearby Aryan houses. Jews were rushing into the burning building and saving the Holy Scrolls while the hilarious crowd all around jeered at them.

Some Jews risked their lives to save holy objects or to keep stormtroopers out of synagogues. Herta Mansbacher, the assistant principal of the Jewish school in Worms, helped to extinguish a fire in the stately Worms Synagogue. When thugs came to start a new fire, she blocked the entrance, but stormtroopers shoved her aside. Flames consumed that synagogue, like so many others. In Jewish cemeteries, Nazis ripped tombstones from the ground and marked them with swastikas.

Bonfires raged throughout Germany, fueled by Jewish religious books and sacred objects. Nazis and their sympathizers stepped on the Holy Scrolls and tossed them in the air. Looters snatched up the velvet covers and silver trimmings from these scrolls, laughing at the helpless rage and sorrow of Jews who stood watching nearby.

Major Synagogues
Destroyed in Towns
in "Greater Germany,"
November 9–10, 1938

Broken Lives

Because the streets were filled with shattered glass, the night of November 9–10 became known as *Kristallnacht*—"Crystal Night," or "Night of Broken Glass." Nobody is sure how many people perished that night, but possibly hundreds, perhaps thousands, were killed throughout Greater Germany.

After *Kristallnacht*, approximately 30,000 Jewish men were forcibly taken to concentration camps—Dachau, Buchenwald, Sachsenhausen, and others. There, prisoners were forced into hard labor. Some were tortured. At least 1,000 were killed, 244 of them at Buchenwald. Men who were able to buy their freedom returned sickly and thin, often with injuries.

Sixty-two Jews were taken to Sachsenhausen. A London newspaper reported that, upon arriving, they were forced to run through a line of SS guards armed with clubs, whips, and spades. They were attacked from all sides and beaten for half an hour. Twelve men were killed, while the others, all left unconscious, suffered serious injuries.

Emil Carlebach, who had been imprisoned at Buchenwald since 1934 for politically opposing the Nazis, later told what happened to the Jews there. He explained that Captain Wolf, a war hero, was hung on the camp's main gate until he died. Waving whips, the SS guards, accompanied by their dogs, terrorized the barracks where the prisoners were trying to sleep at night, smashing men's skulls.

Witnesses noted with particular distress how the Nazis who perpetrated such acts showed no sign of compassion for their victims, nor any remorse. Rabbi Georg Wilde, who spent 11 days at Buchenwald, described sadistic acts. He said that SS men coated steps with soap, then beat the prisoners who slipped. On the way to the camp, they slammed people's heads against the sides of trucks. Prisoners who cried out while being beaten were punished with more blows. Wilde said:

> I realized that these eighteen-year-old or twenty-three-year-old boys were being systematically trained to display brutality towards everyone in the execution of their orders, whether young or old, innocent or guilty.

Even Less Freedom

Attacks on Jews only intensified after *Kristallnacht*. New laws forbade them to own any valuables, radios, or pets. They were also forbidden to use telephones, go to barbers or beauty salons, or to buy foods that were being rationed. Jewish children were formally expelled from public schools. The Nazis also intensified their persecution of Romani, who were ordered to register with the police early in December.

"A World Problem"

Although the German media called *Kristallnacht* "a spontaneous outbreak of the people's rage," most Germans did not take an active part in the violence. Most stayed at home or stood by. A few brought victims into their homes and helped them to clean up. A carpenter who was repairing doors on November 10 remarked, "What a disgrace. It makes you ashamed to be a German." Another man said to his fellow citizens, "Once upon a time, looters were shot; now the police protect them. That's what Germany's come to."

Although some clergy had been sentenced to death for opposing Hitler, a few spoke out. In Swabia, during a sermon, Pastor Julius von Jan denounced the violence and unjust arrests. He said, "Houses of worship, sacred to others, have been burned down with impunity. . . . Our nation's infamy is bound to bring about Divine punishment." In Berlin, Provost Bernhard Lichtenberg of the Catholic Church also condemned *Kristallnacht*:

What took place yesterday, we know; what will be tomorrow, that we do not know; but what happens today, that we have witnessed outside. . . the synagogue is burning, and that also is a house of God.

Journalists and foreign diplomats had witnessed the savagery of that night, and many wrote stories, editorials, and articles expressing their contempt. Sir George Ogilvie-Forbes, a British diplomat in Berlin, warned his government about the danger confronting the Jews:

Misery and despair are already there, and when their resources are either denied to them or exhausted, their end will be starvation. The Jews of Germany are, indeed, not a national but a world problem, which, if neglected, contains the seeds of a terrible vengeance.

At a press conference, U.S. president Franklin D. Roosevelt said, "I myself could scarcely believe that such things could occur in a twentieth-century civilization." Yet, the United States did not change its immigration policy to admit more Jews.

As a further insult, the government ordered Jews to repair all the damage done during *Kristallnacht* with their own money. Insurance companies had to pay the Nazi government the money that they owed to Jewish policyholders for the damage. The

Nazis also fined German Jews the equivalent of about $400 million as a punishment for vom Rath's death. Bank accounts were frozen; Jews could withdraw just a small amount of money each month.

By the end of 1938, Europe's remaining Jews lived in continual fear. Many more Jews decided to leave Germany. In Stuttgart, some 110,000 people applied each month for the 850 exit visas that were available. In Berlin, Captain Frank Foley, head of the British Passport Control Office, begged his government to let thousands enter Palestine. Some people came daily to see whether their emigration papers were ready. Often, they were made to wait for hours in the bitter cold. Foley's office dispensed hot tea, but he was helpless to provide the visas these people desperately needed.

By the end of 1938, the number of Jews in Germany had dropped from approximately 500,000 to about 350,000—about 70 percent of the population from 1933. Most had emigrated, but well over 1,000 had been murdered. Tens of thousands were trapped in concentration camps, which now included Osthofen, Buchenwald, Dachau, Flossenburg, Mauthausen, Ravensbrück, and Sachsenhausen.

An article in the November 23, 1938, issue of a Nazi newspaper, *Das Schwartze Korps,* contained these chilling words:

> *As early as 1933, the year in which we took power, we claimed that the Jewish Question should be solved with the most brutal methods and completely. We were right then but we were not able to implement our view because we lacked the military strength we possess today. It is essential, it is inevitable. We no longer hear the whining of the world. No power on earth can now keep us from bringing the Jewish Question to its total solution.*

As 1938 ended, top Nazi officials called it a decisive year. According to Foreign Minister Joachim von Ribbentrop, 1938 was "the year of our destiny," in which Germany had made "a major step towards the solution of the Jewish problem." Under Adolf Hitler, Nazi Germany had built up its military, brazenly claiming

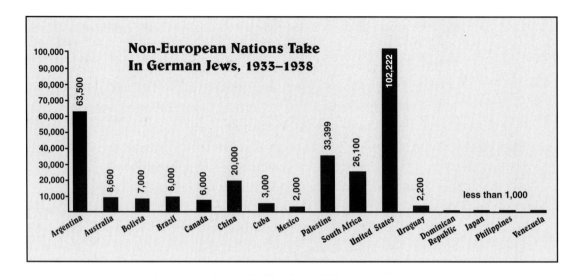

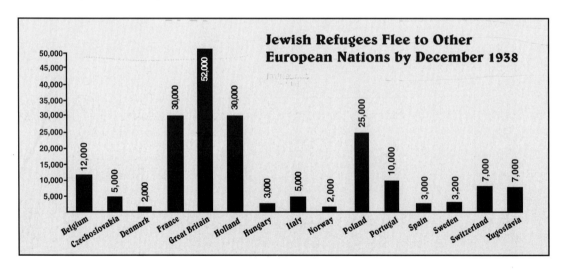

more land and defying international law. The government had
tremendous support—millions of Germans stood eager to follow
Hitler. Nazi Germany would now plunge the world into the dead-
liest war in history. At the same time, Nazis would wage a new
campaign, one of unspeakable cruelty, against millions of inno-
cent civilians.

CHRONOLOGY OF THE HOLOCAUST: 1933–1945

1933

January 30
Adolf Hitler becomes chancellor of Germany

February 28
Nazis declare emergency after Reichstag fire; consolidate power

March 22
Nazis open first concentration camp: Dachau

May 10
Public book burnings target works by Jews and opponents of the Nazis

July 14
Nazi Party established as one and only legal party in Germany ••▶

1934

January 26
German–Polish non-aggression pact signed ••▶

1935

September 15
Nuremberg Laws passed ••▶

1936

March
Germany occupies Rhineland, flouting the Versailles Treaty

August
Olympic Games held in Berlin

1938

November 9–10
Kristallnacht: long-planned pogrom explodes across "Greater Germany"

September 29
Munich Conference: appeasement; Allies grant Germany Sudetenland (part of Czechoslovakia)

July 6–13
Evian Conference: refugee policies

March 13
Anschluss: annexation of Austria

1937

September 7
Hitler declares end of the Versailles Treaty ◀••••

1939

May
British White Paper: Jewish emigration to Palestine limited ••▶

August 23
Soviet–German non-aggression pact signed

September 1
Germany invades Poland; Poland falls within a month

September 2
Great Britain and France declare war on Germany

September 17
Red (Soviet) Army invades eastern Poland

October 8
First ghetto established in Poland

1941

June 22
Operation Barbarossa: invasion of the Soviet Union; German war on two fronts

March 24
Germany invades North Africa

1940

October 16
Order for creation of Warsaw ghetto ◀•••

April 27
Heinrich Himmler orders creation of Auschwitz concentration camp; established May 20

Spring
Germany conquers Denmark, Norway, Belgium, Luxembourg, Holland, and France (occupies northern part)

February 12
Deportation of Jews from Germany to occupied Poland begins

July 31
Reinhard Heydrich appointed to implement "Final Solution": extermination of European Jewry

December 7
Japan attacks Pearl Harbor

December 11
Germany and Italy declare war on the United States ••▶

1942

January 20
Wannsee Conference: coordination of "Final Solution"

Spring–Summer
Liquidation of Polish ghettos; deportation of Jews to extermination camps

November 19–20
Soviet Army counterattacks at Stalingrad

1944

May–July
Deportation of Hungarian Jews: 437,402 sent to Auschwitz

June 6
D-Day: Allies invade Normandy

July
Soviet troops liberate Majdanek camp in Poland ••▶

October 2
Danes rescue more than 7,200 Jews from Nazis ◀•••

June 11
Heinrich Himmler orders liquidation of all ghettos in Poland and the Soviet Union

April 19–May 16
Warsaw ghetto uprising

April 19
Bermuda Conference: fruitless discussion of rescue of Jewish victims of Nazis; liquidation of Warsaw ghetto begins

1943

January 18–21
Major act of resistance in Warsaw ghetto ◀••••

1945

January 27
Soviet troops liberate Auschwitz–Birkenau

April–May
Allies liberate Buchenwald, Bergen-Belsen, Dachau, Mauthausen, and Theresienstadt concentration camps

April 30
Hitler commits suicide

May 7
Germany surrenders unconditionally to Allies

May 8
V-E Day: Victory in Europe

November
Nuremberg Trials begin

Glossary

Anschluss The German invasion and annexation of Austria on March 12–13, 1938.

Anti-Semite A person who hates Jews.

Antisemitism Hatred of Jews.

Aryanization A term used by the Nazis to mean the transfer of all assets and control of German-owned businesses to Germans who were considered Aryans.

Aryans Originally, a term referring to speakers of any Indo-European language. The Nazis used the term to mean people of Northern European background, or members of what the Nazis termed the German "master race."

Communism A political, social, and economic ideology that aims for a classless society. German Communists were the first opponents of the Nazis.

Concentration Camps Labor camps set up by the Nazis to house political prisoners or people they considered to be "undesirable." Prisoners were made to work like slaves and many died as a result of starvation, disease, or beatings. *Also called work camps, work centers, and prison camps.*

Einsatzgruppen "Special Action Groups" or killing squads. Part of the SS, their main purpose was to kill enemies of the Reich, especially Jews and Communists.

Extermination Camps Death camps built by the Nazis in German-occupied Poland for the sole purpose of killing "enemies" of the Third Reich. The victims' bodies were usually burned in ovens (crematoria). The six extermination camps were Auschwitz–Birkenau, Belzec, Chelmno, Majdanek, Sobibór, and Treblinka. *Also called killing centers.*

Fascism A political philosophy or system that values a nation, and often a particular group, above the individual; and that has an autocratic, centralized government, usually headed by a dictator.

Führer A German word meaning "leader." It was used to refer to Adolf Hitler, dictator of Germany from 1933 to 1945 and head of the Nazi Party.

Gentile A non-Jewish person.

Gestapo The Nazi secret police, who were responsible for rounding up, arresting, and deporting victims to ghettos or camps. The Gestapo were part of the SS.

Ghetto In Hitler's Europe, the section of a city where Jews were forced to live apart from other groups, in conditions of extreme crowding and deprivation.

Haganah An underground Jewish defense group from Palestine.

Holocaust A term for the state-sponsored, systematic persecution and annihilation of European Jewry by Nazi Germany and its collaborators between 1933 and 1945. While Jews were the primary victims, with approximately 6 million murdered, many other groups were targeted, including Romani, the mentally and physically disabled, Soviet prisoners of war, political dissidents, Jehovah's Witnesses, and male homosexuals. It is believed that perhaps 4 million non-Jews were killed under the Nazi regime.

Horst Wessel An anthem of the Nazi Party that contained lyrics glorifying the killing of Jews.

Jew A person with a Jewish mother or someone who has converted to Judaism.

Kristallnacht "Night of Broken Glass," or "Crystal Night." November 9–10, 1938, a night of Nazi-planned terror throughout Greater Germany, when Jews were attacked and arrested and their property destroyed.

Lebensraum A German term for "living space" to accommodate what the Nazis called the "master race" of Aryan people.

Mein Kampf In English, "My Struggle." A book written by Adolf Hitler while he was in prison in 1924, in which he outlined his plans for Germany.

Munich Pact A treaty by which Great Britain and France agreed not to resist Germany's occupation of Sudetenland in 1938. *Also called Munich Agreement.*

Mischlinge A derogatory Nazi term meaning "mongrels" or "hybrids" that denoted people having both Christian and Jewish ancestors.

Nazi A member of the Nazi Party or something associated with the party, such as "Nazi government."

Nazi Party Short for the National Socialist German Workers' Party. Founded in 1919, the party became a potent political force under Hitler's leadership.

Nuremberg Laws "Reich Citizenship Laws," passed on September 15, 1935. These sweeping laws specified the qualifications for German citizenship and specifically excluded from citizenship persons of Jewish ancestry.

Palestine A region in the Middle East, part of which is now known as Israel. Palestine was controlled by the British government from 1922 to 1948.

Pogroms Organized, mass attacks against a people. Carried out by the Nazis against those they considered inferior, particularly Jews.

Propaganda The deliberate spreading of ideas, information or rumors—often false—for the purpose of helping or injuring a cause, organization, or person.

Reichstag The German Parliament.

Rhineland A region between Germany and France that was demilitarized after World War I as a buffer zone to prevent another German invasion.

Swastika An ancient design that the Nazis adapted for their party symbol.

SA From the German term *Sturmabteilungen,* meaning "stormtroopers." The SA were Nazi soldiers. *Also called brown-shirts.*

SS From the German term *Schutzstaffel,* meaning "defense unit." The SS began as Hitler's personal bodyguard and developed into the most powerful and feared organization in the Third Reich. *Also called black-shirts.*

Star of David The six-pointed star that is a symbol of Judaism.

Sudetenland The western part of Czechoslovakia along the border of Germany that was invaded and occupied by Germany in 1938.

Third Reich *Reich* means "empire." In German history, the First Reich lasted from 962 until 1806, the second from 1871 to 1918. In the early 1920s, Hitler began using the term "Third Reich" to describe his own empire, which lasted from 1933 until 1945.

Treaty of Versailles The 1919 peace treaty that ended World War I. In it, the conditions of surrender for Germany and the other Axis powers were outlined.

Untermenschen A German word meaning "subhumans," used by the Nazis to refer to some groups they considered "undesirable"—Jews, Romani, male homosexuals, political opponents, and the physically and mentally disabled.

Volkisch A "people's movement" based on a fear and hatred of foreigners, particularly Jews, and that believed in the superiority of the Germanic race.

Source Notes

Introduction:

page 11: "We are the result…." Robert Goldston. *The Life and Death of Nazi Germany.* New York: Fawcett, 1967, p. 13.

page 13: "Every day the people were fed…." Max Von Der Grun. Trans. Jan Van Heurk. *Howl Like the Wolves: Growing Up in Nazi Germany.* New York: William Morrow, 1980, p. 89.

page 15: Material about use of mathematics problems from Seymour Rossel. *The Holocaust.* New York: Franklin Watts, 1981, p. 28.

page 16: "Hatred, burning hatred…." Barbara Rogasky. *Smoke and Ashes.* New York: Holiday House, 1988, p. 20.

page 16: "He was an enormously strong…." David A. Adler. *We Remember the Holocaust.* New York: Henry Holt, 1989, p. 5.

page 16: "a sin against your German Volk…." Editorial: "Finish Up With the Jews." *The SA Man,* 1935, part of the International Military Tribunal Nuremberg Document PS 30–50.

page 17: "rooted in Germany and its culture"; "work not only…." Leonard Baker. *Days of Sorrow and Pain: Leo Baeck and the Berlin Jews.* New York: Macmillan, 1978, p. 172.

page 17: "persecuting Jews could damage…." Baker, pp. 173–174.

Chapter 1:

page 20: Hitler's racial views have been described in various sources, including Abba Eban. *Heritage: Civilization and the Jews.* New York: Summit Books, 1984, p. 302.

page 20: "Marriages between Jews and citizens of German or related blood…." Leni Yahil. *The Holocaust: The Fate of European Jewry.* New York: Oxford University Press, 1990, p. 71.

page 21: "All of a sudden...." Elaine Landau. *We Survived the Holocaust*. New York: Franklin Watts, 1991, pp. 31–32.

page 22: "I did not want...." Carol Rittner and John K. Roth, eds. *Different Voices: Women and the Holocaust*. New York: Paragon House, 1993, p. 194.

page 22: "Don't come in...." Rittner and Roth, p. 194.

page 23: "complete disinheritance...." Martin Gilbert. *The Holocaust*. New York: Oxford University Press, 1986, p. 48.

page 23: "While before I went to Germany...." Gilbert. *The Holocaust*. p. 49.

page 24: "When we were seated, he said...." Rittner and Roth, p. 195.

page 24: "All weakness must be hammered out...." Von Der Grun, p. 117.

page 24: "These young people will learn nothing else...." Von Der Grun, pp. 118–119.

pages 24–25: "I must say I liked it..." and "It was an advantage to join...." Arnold P. Rubin. *The Evil That Men Do: The Story of the Nazis*. New York: Julian Messner, 1977, p. 63.

page 25: "It is quite possible for a people...." Quoted in Max Von Der Grun, p. 99.

page 26: "The only thing to do...." Baker, p. 180.

page 26: "We stand before our God...." Baker, p. 206.

page 26: "...any government which permits...." Baker, p. 208.

page 26: "I will go...." Baker, p. 238.

Chapter 2:

page 31: "I...had packs...." Rubin, p. 111.

page 32: "One could forget...." Baker, p. 185.

page 32: Cecilia Bernstein quoted in Adler, p. 23.

page 33: "inhuman indifferences" and "reach the hearts of men...." Quoted in Gilbert, *The Holocaust*. p. 53.

Chapter 3:

page 36: Gretel Bergmann quoted in Robert Slater. *Great Jews in Sports*. Middle Village, NY: Jonathan David Publishers, 1983, p. 26.

page 37: "a little dark man with a comic-opera mustache..." Tony Gentry, *Jesse Owens*. New York: Chelsea House, 1990, p. 13.

page 38: "Do you really think...." Gentry. p. 65.

page 38: "We used to play...." Von Der Grun, p. 107.

page 39: "I wrack my brains...." Friedrich Percyval Reck-Malleczewen. Trans. by Paul Rubens. *Diary of a Man in Despair*. London: Collier-Macmillan, 1970, p. 22.

page 39: "height of shame" and "incapable any longer of perceiving its shame for the shame that it is." Reck-Malleczewen, p. 23.

page 39: "no human being" and "set fire to the world." Reck-Malleczewen, p. 26.

Chapter 4:

page 42: "It would mean the end of...." Alexander Stille. *Benevolence and Betrayal: Five Italian Jewish Families Under Fascism*. New York: Simon & Schuster, 1991, p. 55.

page 42: "fascism is a regime...." Stille, p. 55.

page 42: "[Hitler] is an idiot...." Stille, p. 55.

page 43: "I was very proud...." Stille, p. 69.

page 43: "...We started crying...." Stille, p. 70.

pages 43–44: "My father was not able...." Stille, p. 77.

page 44: "Most of our friends...." Stille, p. 71.

page 48: "No more will we keep silent...." Martin Niemöller. *The Gestapo Defied*. London: William Hodge, 1941, p. 54.

page 49: "World opinion will stop Hitler...." and "It won't happen here." Clara Isaacman as told to Joan Adess Grossman. *Clara's Story*. Philadelphia: The Jewish Publication Society, 1984, p. 2.

Chapter 5:

page 53: Quotes from Shirer in William L. Shirer. *The Nightmare Years: 1930–1940*. Boston: Little, Brown, 1984, p. 314.

page 54: "I heard marching boots...." Adler, p. 20.

page 54: "At the end of March 1938...." Adler, p. 29.

page 54: "all of us were soon stunned...." Miep Gies with Alison Leslie Gold. *Anne Frank Remembered: The Story of the Woman Who Helped to Hide the Frank Family*. New York: Simon and Schuster, 1987, p. 40.

page 56: "that boundaries exist...." Reck-Malleczewen, p. 58.

page 56: "As we have no...." Quoted in Gilbert, *Atlas of the Holocaust*, p. 64.

page 57: "There is one ideal...." Ehud Avriel. *Open the Gates! The Dramatic Personal Story of "Illegal" Immigration to Israel*. New York: Atheneum, 1975, p. 27.

page 60: "peace for our time." Robert T. Elson and the Editors of Time-Life Books. *Prelude to War*. New York: Time-Life Books, 1976, p. 198.

Chapter 6:

page 64: "in the name of twelve thousand...." Quoted in Rita Thalmann and Emmanuel Feinermann. Trans. by Gilles Cremonesi. *Crystal Night: 9–10 November 1938*. New York: Coward, McCann, and Geoghegan, 1974, p. 25.

page 65: "Preparations...." Quoted in Thalmann and Feinermann, p. 59.

page 65: "We shall no longer tolerate...." Quoted in Thalmann and Feinermann, p. 56.

page 66: "axe blows...." Engelmann, p. 130.

page 66: "I heard a cupboard...." Engelmann, pp. 130–131.

page 67: "The fire brigade...." Quoted in Seymour Rossel. *The Holocaust*. New York: Franklin Watts, 1981, p. 35.

page 69: "I realized that these eighteen-year-old...." Thalmann and Feinermann, pp. 128–129.

page 70: "a spontaneous outbreak...." Stadtler, p. 13.

page 70: "What a disgrace...." Engelmann, p. 137.

page 70: "Once upon a time...." Engelmann, p. 138.

page 70: "Houses of worship...." Quoted in Martin Gilbert, *The Holocaust*, p. 73.

page 70: "What took place yesterday...." Yehuda Bauer. *The Holocaust in Historical Perspective*. Seattle: University of Washington Press, 1978, p. 136.

page 70: "Misery and despair...." Rubin, p. 70.

page 70: "I myself could scarcely...." Roosevelt's statement appears in OF76c, Box 6, President's Official File, Roosevelt Library, Hyde Park, NY.

page 71: "As early as 1933...." Avriel, p. 65.

page 71: "the year of our destiny...." Thalmann and Feinermann, p. 11.

Bibliography

David A. Adler. *We Remember the Holocaust*. New York: Henry Holt, 1989.

David Altshuler. *Hitler's War Against the Jews*. New York: Behrman House, 1978.

Ehud Avriel. *Open the Gates! The Dramatic Personal Story of 'Illegal' Immigration to Israel*. New York: Atheneum, 1975.

Edith Baer. *A Frost in the Night: Girlhood on the Eve of the Third Reich*. New York: Pantheon, 1980.

Leonard Baker. *Days of Sorrow and Pain: Leo Baeck and the Berlin Jews*. New York: Macmillan, 1978.

Yehuda Bauer. *A History of the Holocaust*. New York: Franklin Watts, 1982.

Yehuda Bauer. *The Holocaust in Historical Perspective*. Seattle: University of Washington Press, 1978.

Miriam Chaikin. *A Nightmare in History: The Holocaust, 1933–1945*. New York: Clarion, 1987.

Lucy Dawidowicz. *The War Against the Jews, 1933–1945*. New York: Holt, Rinehart, and Winston, 1975.

John V H. Dippel. *Bound Upon A Wheel of Fire: Why So Many German Jews Made the Tragic Decision to Remain in Nazi Germany*. New York: HarperCollins, 1996.

Abba Eban. *Heritage: Civilization and the Jews*. New York: Summit Books, 1984.

Robert T. Elson and the Editors of Time-Life Books. *Prelude to War*. New York: Time-Life Books, 1976.

Bernt Engelmann. *In Hitler's Germany: Everyday Life in the Third Reich*. New York: Alfred Knopf, 1986.

Saul Friedländer. *Nazi Germany and the Jews: The Years of Persecution 1933–1939*. London: Weidenfeld & Nicolson, 1997.

Ina B. Friedman. *The Other Victims: First-Person Stories of Non-Jews Persecuted by the Nazis*. Boston: Houghton-Mifflin, 1990.

Martin Gilbert. *The Fate of the Jews in Nazi Europe*. New York: Mayflower, 1979.

Martin Gilbert. *The Holocaust*. New York: Oxford University Press, 1986.

Martin Gilbert. *The Macmillan Atlas of the Holocaust*. New York: Macmillan, 1982.

Daniel Jonah Goldhagen. *Hitler's Willing Executioners: Ordinary Germans and the Holocaust*. New York: Knopf, 1996.

Robert Goldston. *The Life and Death of Nazi Germany*. New York: Fawcett, 1967.

Frederic Grunfeld. *The Hitler File*. New York: Random House, 1974.

Allen Guttman. *The Olympics: A History of the Games*. Champaign-Urbana: University of Illinois Press, 1992.

Raul Hilberg. *The Destruction of the European Jews*. Rev. ed. 3 vols. New York: Holmes and Meier, 1985.

Clara Isaacman, as told to Joan Adess Grossman. *Clara's Story*. Philadelphia: The Jewish Publication Society, 1984.

H.W Koch. *The Hitler Youth: Origins and Development, 1922–1945*. New York: Stein and Day, 1975.

Nora Levin. *The Holocaust: The Destruction of European Jewry, 1933–1945*. New York: Crowell, 1968.

Richard D. Mandel. *The Nazi Olympics*. New York: Macmillan, 1971.

Michael R. Marrus. *The Holocaust in History*. Hanover and London: University Press of New England, 1987.

Milton Meltzer. *Never to Forget: The Jews of the Holocaust*. New York: Harper & Row, 1976.

Judith Miller. *One By One By One: Facing the Holocaust*. New York: Simon and Schuster, 1990.

Friedrich Percyval Reck-Malleczewen. *Diary of a Man in Despair*. Trans. by Paul Rubens. London: Collier-Macmillan, 1970.

Carol Rittner and John K. Roth, eds. *Different Voices: Women and the Holocaust*. New York: Paragon House, 1993.

Sylvia Rothchild, ed. *Voices From the Holocaust*. New York: New American Library, 1981.

William L. Shirer. *Berlin Diary*. New York: Alfred A. Knopf, 1941.

William L. Shirer. *The Nightmare Years: 1930–1940*. Boston: Little, Brown, and Co., 1984.

William L. Shirer. *The Rise and Fall of the Third Reich*. New York: Simon and Schuster, 1960.

Robert Slater. *Great Jews in Sports*. Middle Village, NY: Jonathan David Publishers, Inc., 1983.

Alexander Stille. *Benevolence and Betrayal: Five Italian Jewish Families Under Fascism*. New York: Simon & Schuster, 1991.

Rita Thalmann and Emmanuel Feinermann. *Crystal Night: 9–10 November 1938*. Trans. Gilles Cremonesi. New York: Coward, McCann, and Geoghegan, 1974.

Isaiah Trunk. *Jewish Responses to Nazi Persecution*. New York: Stein & Day, 1979.

Max Von Der Grun. *Howl Like the Wolves: Growing Up in Nazi Germany*. Trans. Jan Van Heurk. New York: William Morrow, 1980.

Leni Yahil. *The Holocaust: The Fate of European Jewry*. New York: Oxford University Press, 1991.

Further Reading

David A. Adler. *We Remember the Holocaust*. New York: Henry Holt, 1989.

Miriam Chaikin. *A Nightmare in History: The Holocaust, 1933–1945*. New York: Clarion, 1987.

Anne Frank. *The Diary of a Young Girl*. The Definitive Edition. New York: Doubleday, 1995.

Ina B. Friedman. *Escape or Die: True Stories of Young People Who Survived the Holocaust*. Reading, MA: Addison-Wesley, 1982.

Ina B. Friedman. *The Other Victims: First-Person Stories of Non-Jews Persecuted by the Nazis*. Boston: Houghton-Mifflin, 1990.

Allan Guttman. *The Olympics: A History of the Games*. Champaign-Urbana: University of Illinois Press, 1992.

Clara Isaacman, as told to Joan Adess Grossman. *Clara's Story*. Philadelphia: The Jewish Publication Society, 1984.

H. W. Koch. *The Hitler Youth: Origins and Development, 1922–1945*. New York: Stein and Day, 1975.

Milton Meltzer. *Never to Forget: The Jews of the Holocaust*. New York: Harper & Row, 1976.

Robert Slater. *Great Jews in Sports*. Middle Village, NY: Jonathan David Publishers, 1983.

Max Von Der Grun. *Howl Like the Wolves: Growing Up in Nazi Germany*. Trans. Jan Van Heurk. New York: William Morrow, 1980.

Index

Photo Credits

Cover and pages 55, 56, 67: National Archives, courtesy of USHMM Photo Archives; pages 8, 9: Richard Freimark, courtesy of USHMM Photo Archives; page 15: Library of Congress; pages 18, 19: Blackbirch Press Photo Archives; page 20: Marion Davy, courtesy of USHMM Photo Archives; page 22 (top): Abraham Pisarek/Bildarchiv Abraham Pisarek, courtesy of USHMM Photo Archives; pages 22 (bottom), 27: Bildarchiv Preussicher Kulturbesitz, courtesy of USHMM Photo Archives; pages 28, 29, 40, 41: YIVO Institute for Jewish Research, courtesy of USHMM Photo Archives; pages 32, 57: courtesy of USHMM Photo Archives; pages 34, 35, 39, 61: AP/Wide World Photos; pages 47, 64: KZ Gedenkstatte Dachau, courtesy of USHMM Photo Archives; page 50, 51: Oesterreichische Gesellschaft Fur Zeitgeschichte, courtesy of USHMM Photo Archives; page 59: National Archives; page 63, 64: American Jewish Archives, courtesy of USHMM Photo Archives.
Maps and graphs ©Blackbirch Press, Inc.

PLEASE!

DO NOT REMOVE
THE DATE DUE CARD
FROM THIS POCKET.

THERE IS A $1.00
FINE IF YOU LOSE IT!